Beyond
the Prison
of Beliefs

Where Science Meets Spirit

A.A. LOTFY

Beyond the Prison of Beliefs:

Where Science Meets Spirit

A. A. Lotfy

ISBN (Print Edition): 978-1-54396-836-1

ISBN (eBook Edition): 978-1-54396-837-8

Ahmed A. Lotfy
San Stefano, Alexandria, Egypt

info@ahmedalotfy.com

Table of Contents

BACKGROUND

A hmed A. Lotfy holds a bachelor of science in computer science from the American University of Kuwait. He completed his master's in business administration from Maastricht School of Management. A. A. Lotfy is a behavioral and spiritual enthusiast who spent a significant period of his life learning about, and probing into comparative religion, physics, psychology, and social & behavioral sciences. He has acquired a Myers-Briggs Type Indicator (MBTI) Steps I and II license, and his life is mostly dedicated to the mysterious world of quantum physics and its connection with human beings on a molecular, spiritual, and behavioral level. A.A.Lotfy is also a vice curator in the Global Shapers Community, Doha Hub; a World Economic Forum initiative, targeted to shape the environment, and people so we could contribute to a promising future.

ACKNOWLEDGMENTS

Beyond the Prison of Beliefs was an extraordinary journey of discovery not just reflecting the various topics that I personally found captivating, but it was an intriguing trip into the deepest and darkest corners of my personality, mind, and soul. This journey made me challenge myself in many different ways that revealed and peeled layers I didn't know existed. It's only through adversities one can grow. Just like carbon before it turns to diamond, it undertakes a towering amount of pressure from everything around it. And suddenly, something breaks open, and there is a deep molecular shift. The same thing happens to humans. Before we experience this vast shift in our lives, it feels like the toughest, heaviest, most intense experience ever. Before we break open, it feels like everything around us is pulling us down, weighing on us, and squeezing the life out of us in a very painful manner. Only then you will be able to experience deep liberation, joy, and unconditional love. We are all in a never-ending learning expedition on the voyage of life, and *this* one, so far, was the most significant phase to me. You may not know that you were the main trigger and reason why I decided to write this book…Hana. For that, I owe you a lot.

Furthermore, I would like to acknowledge my second family, Mrs. Noha, Syed, Dina, Angel, Dr. Bendriss, and Dr. Marco. They made leaving home feel seamless and are all pleasant and accomplished professionals that I am honored to work with. This book might never have happened if I hadn't been given the space for personal growth and professional development. I am also immensely grateful for Dr. Mohammed Elshazly, Dr. Mohamud Verjee, and Mr. Ghanim Al-Sulaiti dedicating some of their precious time and going out of their way to help me out.

I want to acknowledge the person I truly admire and consider an angelic spirit, guiding me as a divine presence from heaven: my uncle Ahmed Shawky, may his soul rest in peace. I would also like to thank his wife, Dr. Hanan, who deftly made it into the hearts of my family, as well as my two amazing cousins, Shawky and Abdelrahman. I want to show much gratitude to the person responsible for raising me through childhood, always being patient with me and accepting of who I am, my lovely and elegant grandmother, Kamilia. I would especially like to thank my magnificent aunt, Dr. Nivine, for genuinely treating me as a second son; likewise, I view her as a mother and an exceptional leader. I would also like to thank her husband and my second father, Dr. Alaa, who always opened his home to me as much as to his children; and my second brother and sisters, Dr. Ali, Dr. Basant, and Dr. Dalia respectively.

A special thank you to my gracious, loving brother, Amr, the better half of me, and the one person I rely on the most.

Finally, I cannot express how much I owe my outstanding parents for shaping me into the person I am today, the by-product of their efforts. My sincerest gratitude to my fantastic idol and support in life, my chivalrous father, Dr. Abdelrahman, for being a role model in generosity, wisdom, compassion, and selflessness. I am forever in debt to him for that. And most importantly, the person who is not just an extension of who I am, but also the most caring, relentless figure who never ceased to shy away from anything that made me a better and happier person (even when it meant taking away a piece of hers), my sweet and beautiful mother, Howaida.

INTRODUCTION

Science without religion is lame,
religion without science is blind.

— Albert Einstein

What is the purpose of existence? Are we free spiritual beings? What is the essence of the soul? Is there more to the universe than the eyes can see? Where is God? Does He exist? Are science and religion two different things, or are they one? All these questions are overwhelmingly complex to answer; they are mysterious enigmas that have long baffled the human mind and made each one of us question reality at a particular stage of our lives. Arguably, every person has had at least one of these paradoxes occupy a notable amount of their time and often decided to either ratify or refute their validity. If you're eager to piece together the most mystifying puzzle of all time and bring to light the leading dispute of most human quarrels, disagreements, divisions, hatred, and wars since the beginning of time, then you are already on the right path. The first step one should carry out when confronted with a predicament is to identify the source of the problem. The best approach to fix anything is to figure out what caused the damage to begin with; otherwise, the plight will keep recurring, and history will continue to repeat itself in interminable cycles. In the bigger scheme of things, attaining more comprehensive knowledge is a way to reach a pivotal, universal understanding. It's not about how different we are—that's only a sign of ignorance and how little we know—it's about how much we know and discover about ourselves. Human beings have a lot in common. In a way, we function similarly when given comparable exposure and circumstances. Individuality and uniqueness are nothing but an illusion and a result of our unparalleled experiences in life. The pool of discordant ideologies, belief systems, cultures, social constructs, and societies across the world will either divide us further or unify us over the long haul. This book is not designated for science or religion solely but the overlap between them. I have done my best to neutralize my past viewpoints, present notions, and future outlooks so I can build a foundation on a clean-slated knowledge base of findings, introspections, and truth-seeking. I invite you to do the same. I am not alleging that I have *the answer*; I propose a starting point in the hope that it leads to a common ground of understanding.

Purpose, Destiny.
Where do we come from?
Where will we go?
The most beautiful thing we can experience is the mysterious.
It is the source of all true art and all science.
The true sign of intelligence is not knowledge,
but imagination.
Learn from yesterday.
Live for today.
Hope for tomorrow.

— Neba

CHAPTER 1:
THE AWE-INSPIRING UNIVERSE

*N*ature is beauty. Beauty is nature. We are engineers, but who engineered us? As we scan our universe, from the tiny flower to the awe-inspiring galaxy, we see the fingerprint of a creator, the fingerprint of intelligence. The universe consists entirely of waves of motion which spring from stillness and return to stillness. Nature is designed according to a sequence. This sequence appears to be a trademark of a designer. A proof of a creator, something left behind indicating the one who was there... a finger print. Anahera

Creation of the Universe

There's a sequence to life that has led us to this point, and if you follow the trail of this sequence back, you will find no evidence of anything as intricate as the universe occurring by coincidence or fortuity. Why is it that, when we gaze at the pyramids, we have an understanding that an intelligent ancient civilization had something to do with it? Someone could argue that they came together as a result of sandstorms piling rocks up on top of each other, but that's highly unlikely, of course: there's no room for chance to mount an exquisitely erect monument in such precision. We tend to believe our history regardless of who recorded it, and we deduce the undeniable existence of ancient civilizations even though we haven't personally witnessed any of them. When we visit a museum or a monument, we sporadically inspect the ancient remains in obscurity, and every so often we express our interest in identifying who created the artifact, yet we only link human-made structures with a creator. However, when it comes to nature, be it a flower, animal, mountain, lake, sky, planet, galaxy, or spatial bodies far more complex in constituents than concrete buildings and relics, we argue that it's a spin-off coincidence!

The universe is so intricate in function, design, composition, and beauty, that it makes me susceptible to believe that it's a product of intelligent design rather than a by-product of chance. We are fingerprints of a creator, even if the initiation happened by coincidence; it's still considered a creation, a remarkably accurate and flawless formation! When a scientist oversees an experiment, and the outcome is providently undesirable, it doesn't mean it won't be deemed a sanctioned invention even if a twist of fate was evident. Most groundbreaking discoveries came to pass by accident; many scientists would acknowledge that. The happenstance wouldn't emerge out of oblivion. It's the fundamental rule of any science experiment: studies include an object and a stimulant to be able to induce results—cause and effect. So, whether the blueprint of the universe was providence or luck, it doesn't change the fact that whatever came to existence is nothing less than exemplary. There is perfection in the balance of life, the order within the chaos, and vice versa. Everything is deliberately designed in a way to serve a purpose. There's always a sense of deliberation in the serendipities surrounding us, so what makes the big bang any different than a deliberate act? We are naturally inclined to have suspicions about the design instead of spending that energy to grasp the wisdom behind it. Would you be grateful for the good if there were no bad at all? Would you even fathom what is *good* if *bad* was nonexistent? The tale of Adam and Eve depicts this subject matter thoroughly and proficiently.

The big bang itself is a result of a reaction, but what spawned this reaction? Who triggered it? Aren't we breaching science when we say that it was a reaction set in motion by nothing? A higher power setting it off may strike someone as pseudoscience, yet it's equally (if not more) scientifically skewed to allege that nothing elicited this reaction. With no evidence, we'll find ourselves locking horns to the point of stalemate. Therefore, we must consider a daring leap forward in the direction that makes more sense *scientifically*, until we manage to prove otherwise. The answers will reveal themselves over time. It has always been the case.

Meanwhile, invalidating the opposite likelihood of what you believe is the truth is wrong; one should be receptive to everything. Many theories about the origins of our universe have come and gone until another method came along that physicists could agree on. It's the big bang theory. They decided on it because there is scientific evidence to support it. Georges Lemaître and Alexander Friedmann were the founders of this theory in the 1920s. They used Einstein's theory of relativity to prove that the universe is in a continuous motion of exponential expansion. In 1929, the American astronomer Edwin Hubble reinforced this theory after discerning evidence that practically all clusters of near and distant galaxies seemed to be moving away from all other clusters, which also betokens that the entire universe is expanding. In chapter 51, verse 47, the Quran affirms "And it is We [God] who have built the universe with [Our creative] power and verily, it is We [God] who are steadily expanding it." The emerging universe expanded from an infinitely dense point of singularity, which was very unstable, so it exploded as blistering gravitational waves. One thing we are informed about the universe is that space was formed first and then gave birth to galaxies, stars, planets, the Earth, and then us. The Quran addresses the order in which numerous events took place in a consistent alignment with scientific findings. For instance, in chapter 18, verse 51 it says "I [God] did not make them witness to the creation of the heavens and the earth or to the creation of themselves." That implies that the order of creation was space, Earth, and then us respectively.

The archetypical bedtime stories of the beginning of time, of sanctified heroes and revered messengers, were illustrated in a way to feed our human imagination and to gradually assimilate the prowess of the divine. They are just analogies to put strenuous matters into perspective because what is real cannot be set in words. We cannot pump faith into a three-year-old child by explaining quantum physics to them. Alternatively, we adhere to Disney metaphors to drill in concepts of morality. The human mind was wittingly devised to relate to figurative imaginations. We are prone to gravitate toward miraculous affinities. The reality about the truth is not in the stories conveyed but in the means of interpretation.

Another mind-boggling controversy is what existed before the big bang. What will we find if we go back infinitely into the time preceding the big bang? These questions will compel us to reflect on the verisimilitude of time and life as we know it. Let's consider that the big bang was an erratic act of mere chance, and that galaxies and other Milky Ways were formed coincidentally. Stars came into existence, and planets eloquently and gracefully revolved around their host stars. If we pore over planet Earth, what are the chances of it whirling systematically around the sun, at a safe and uniform radius in the Goldilocks zone where the temperature is just about right for the liquid to exist, and thus life also?

The human body is a captivating establishment. The exquisite intricacy of its vital organs and exuberant systems function in unsurpassed consonance that makes one wonder if there was an intelligent mastermind, and then how impeccable must He be to come up with such a design! It doesn't matter if it was evolution that led us here: evolution is still an act of a pristine creator. Many call our creator *God*. The indoctrinated concept of God varies from one person to another. Some refer to Him as the highest power and the source of everything that was created; some refer to Him as intelligence, others refer to Him as everything in existence that is external to us (i.e., the universe), and yet others believe He is everything in existence, *including* us. A manifestation of all consciousness in life! As long as we find meaning in and purpose to our existence, it doesn't matter what our belief is. If we don't find meaning to everything around us, we lose hope and faith, and without faith, there is no reason to live. Not having a desire to live defies human nature. Hope is the pulsating quasar of life.

Faith that life goes on is deeply engraved within our being. It's persistently progressive by nature, and it's the reason evolution supervened in the first place. There is a cogent internal force within every living being that thrusts us forward. A force that drives us onward and outward the same way the big bang surged matter (and antimatter) forward at an accelerating speed. What is this tenacious force that accompanied us to where we are today and is still propelling us to a mysterious future? The unknown is never going to be fully unveiled, nor will it fail to delight.

Space is a vast and dark void governed by an extraordinary power called gravity. Gravity is a force that exists in all material objects in this universe and attracts them toward each other. Without gravity, life on Earth would not exist; the planet would not continue to revolve around the sun and drift in random directions. The moon would float away, the satellite stations would wander aimlessly, and everything on Earth would sail off its surface. When Isaac Newton was relaxing under a tree in his garden, an apple fell on his head, and he deduced that gravity must have been pulling the apple downwards. However, centuries later, Einstein had a different theory: gravity is not pulling us downwards, but rather space is pushing us down. Einstein predicted that through gravity, objects warp the space-time around them as a buoy on water, or a person sitting on a trampoline. The more massive the object, the more it pushes the fabric down. Such movement of every object from a human to a gigantic black hole creates ripples in the space-time continuum. Einstein used this analogy to explain it further: "Just as a boat sailing through the ocean produces waves in the water [ripples], moving masses like stars or black holes produce gravitational waves [ripples] in the fabric of space-time." These ripples set an orbital platform or track on which smaller objects are pulled in a rotational motion around the bigger objects due to the uniform centripetal force (similar to a roulette).

On February 11, 2016, the executive director of the Laser Interferometer Gravitational-Wave Observatory, David Reitze proclaimed that researchers had identified gravitational waves that were generated by the merging of two black holes. This was a

groundbreaking discovery by all means and confirmed the significant foresight of Einstein over one hundred years ago. What's even
more captivating is what the Quran discoursed on gravitational
waves over fourteen hundred years ago. To illustrate what these
gravitational waves are like, Einstein and other physics experts and
professors compared the movement of spatial figures to a child's
bounce on a trampoline. In verse 11 of chapter 86 of the Quran, it is
written "By the heaven which is characterized by its bounce..." The
scripture attests to this bizarre quality function of the heavens, or
space as we generally call it, by referring to the distinct movement: a
bounce produced when heavenly bodies float in space.

Let's take a look at gravity's lesser-known sibling, microgravity.
What pops into your head when the term *astronaut* is mentioned?
Even though a swimmer is not the first thing that would come to
mind, since astronauts fly up into space, did you know that astronauts have to be exceptional swimmers? According to NASA, "...
floating in space is a lot like floating in the water." As a result of this
phenomenon, NASA has built a massive pool that is ten times bigger
than an Olympic-sized one, so their astronauts can practice space
walks by going for a swim. The vast swimming pool is called the
Neutral Buoyancy Laboratory, and it simulates the circumstances
in the gravity-free space. The underground lab carries 6.2 million
gallons of water and is utilized by astronauts in their full space suits
to carry out the duties they will be expected to execute in space.
With the aid of scuba divers, astronauts exercise seven hours in the
swimming pool for every one hour they will spend on a spacewalk.
Interestingly, there is no water in space, yet NASA prepares their
astronauts for those walks in the world's biggest swimming pool.

The Quran associated space with water as well when it stated, "And it is He who created the night and the day and the sun and the moon, All in orbit are swimming." Quran, CH21: V33. The scripture particularly used the analogy of swimming to highlight the micro-gravity and weightless floating environment of space. If space has waves and ripples like water, then what's keeping spatial bodies in place and stopping them from just floating off? It's the gravitational anchors, a term stamped by the physicist Robert Tuttle in 2012. To assimilate this better, the physicists Thomas Van Flandern and Jean-Pierre Vigier came up with a brilliant analogy that explains the transmission of gravitational effects. It suggests we imagine a buoy floating on the surface of the sea. A chain connects the buoy to an anchor that is keeping it in place. If the anchor is removed, the chain causes the buoy to move in random directions. If the anchor is trans-ferred to a different point, the chain causes the buoy to move as well. In return, the buoy's motion sets off waves in the water. If we trans-pose this analogy into gravitational effects, the anchor becomes the source mass, the chain is the gravitational force, and the buoy is the target mass. The waves in the water, originated by the buoy's move-ment and caused by the motion of the anchor, flow in the rippled water and are comparable to gravitational waves.

Research has shown that our sun is the gravitational anchor of the solar system. Furthermore, the black hole at the center of almost every galaxy, including our own, behaves as a gravitational anchor for the galaxies, binding them together in space. When the Quran revealed how the universe was fabricated, it verified that the Earth needs to be anchored by declaring "And He [God] has dropped into the Earth what anchors it, Lest it should shake [shift] with you." Quran, CH16: V15. In a different verse, it is inscribed "He [God] made in the Earth what anchors it from high above." Quran, CH41: V10. It is worth noting that the Quran uses the term *dropped*, and the phrase *from high above it* in these verses; because, in essence, David Reitz proved that gravitational waves from those colliding black holes in space crossed the planet Earth. Lawrence Krauss mentioned in his book, *A Universe from Nothing: Why There Is Something Rather than Nothing*, that the total amount of energy in the universe is equal to exactly zero. This is because the universe's positive energy in the form of matter is scratched out by its negative energy in the form of gravity. In simpler words, gravity balances matter since the net energy of the universe is zero. That implies the universe is virtually nothing. Krauss argues that, if the universe sums up to nothing, then why do we feel coerced to bid a God to justify its cause? The Quran denotes that what anchors the Earth balances everything when it states "We have spread out the Earth, and dropped into Earth what anchors it [gravity] And caused to grow therein of everything [matter] in due balance." Quran, CH15: V19-21. So, let's appreciate this astonishing pull of nature we know as gravity.

*　*　*

The atoms of our bodies are traceable to stars that manufactured them in their cores and exploded these enriched ingredients across our galaxy, billions of years ago. For this reason, we are biologically connected to every other living thing in the world. We are chemically connected to all molecules on Earth. And we are atomically connected to all atoms in the universe. We are not figuratively, but literally stardust.

— Neil deGrasse Tyson

There are two types of universes: the external universe, and the universe within us. Both are congruent with each other. One is expanding outward, and the other is expanding inward, so we are nowhere close to conquering either. The external universe is proliferating exponentially in terms of matter (planets, solar systems, galaxies, milky ways all made up of particles, atoms, electrons, and quarks). The universe within is made out of the same atoms. The further we reach out in space the more we discover the resemblance when we dive inward into the human body. We have not yet reached a stage where we have a full understanding of the human body, brain, heart, and so on. We keep discovering smaller and smaller particles, and the exploration doesn't seem like it's going to end anytime soon. Scientists are predicting that what lies at the very core of every atom is a strand of vibrating energy. If the size of a string were to be compared to a tree, then the human body would analogize the size of the solar system. So, imagine how much time it will take us to eventually reach this strand of energy. There is an infinite space within us, and the most sophisticated technologies can't get hold of its extremities. We invent cutting-edge devices to help us probe into the universe within us, the same way we send spaceships and droids to pioneer the external universe. When we plunge deep into the human body, we discern that at a quantum level the rules of physics break down. Our recent insights into how atoms are governed on a subatomic level are being revised. It appears that we are oblivious when it comes to deciphering physics at a quantum state. Many scientists are bewildered by the fact that quantum laws do not compliment the general laws of physics: this challenges their perception of reality. The world's best scientists put their abilities to the test in order to achieve a unified formula that can consolidate our supposition of reality. The theory of everything is on trial, but we need to fully comprehend what's transpiring in the quantum world before integrating our findings with the macro world.

* * *

Quantum World

Quantum mechanics is certainly imposing. But an inner voice tells me that it is not yet the real thing. The theory says a lot, but does not really bring us any closer to the secret of the old one. I, at any rate, am convinced that He does not throw dice.

—Albert Einstein

Quantum theory is the most challenging theory to spell out. Our understanding of it is finite, and even the best physicists do not have a holistic knowledge of its essence because it's boundless and puzzling to decode, and what is strenuous to unravel is exasperating to clarify. In this chapter, I'll do my best to simplify the terms and explanations by using analogies and examples. That's probably the ideal way to explain the preposterous.

The quantum world is critical because it entails theories that challenge what we already know about reality and methods that led scientists to believe that life is an illusion. Quantum theory explains the physical nature at the smallest scales of energy levels of atoms and subatomic particles. Our understanding of physics, when it comes to atoms that make up solid, liquid, and gas, is straightforward to predict when it comes to their energy levels, vibrations, and position. However, when it comes to subatomic particles that make up these atoms, the behavior changes drastically into something we can't grasp. If you track one subatomic particle under a powerful microscope, you will find its behavior rather bizarre. It won't have a specific energy level that labels it as a solid, liquid, or gas particle! Instead, one instant it will be at point A and the next it will jump to point B with no sighted track, then it will disappear, then reappear at point C. It's an entirely random and chaotic state that does not follow a specific pattern. Now, that's one particle! Imagine a handful of subatomic particles all behaving the same way. These subatomic particles make up atoms, so why aren't they acting like atoms? No one knows: this disintegrates all the ground theories of physics and makes it hard to find a unified equation that governs everything. If the laws of physics don't apply on a subatomic scale, then how can we comprehend our reality?

* * *

Spooky Action at a Distance

All matter originates and exists only by virtue of a force...
We must assume behind this force the existence of a conscious
and intelligent mind. This mind is the matrix of all matter.

— Max Planck

Imagine for a minute that you are a tiny strand of energy, hovering in the universe. Theoretically speaking, there is an identical strand of energy that is intimately connected to you since the day you were born. No matter how much distance separates you, whatever happens to one strand instantaneously affects the other strand. They mirror each other in every way possible. If you're happy, your mirror strand is happy; if you're angry, your mirror strand is angry. This is quantum entanglement. The reason Einstein called it "spooky action at a distance" was because the behavior of one particle instantaneously impacted the other no matter how far apart the particles were. Some bedrock rules of physics suggest that nothing can travel faster than the speed of light, and their immediate surrounding stimuli can only impact objects.

Quantum entanglement breaks the rock-base foundation of physics! So, what is it exactly? Is it a portal to some other dimension? Is it connected to wormholes? Does it have to do with human beings connected on a subatomic level? We cannot eliminate any possibility. So, we are going to examine this phenomenon further from both scientific and religious standpoints. As studies have proven, if you separate two entangled particles and place one on the top of a pyramid in Giza, for instance, and conceal the other particle in the Empire State Building in New York, then spin the particle on top of the pyramid clockwise, its counterpart in the Empire State Building will instantaneously rotate anticlockwise. No matter how much distance stretches between both particles, the corresponding action is instantaneous and doesn't account for time. So, what does that mean? Maybe science cannot provide answers right now, but it is undoubtedly heading in the right direction.

One of the verses in the Quran mentions this phenomenon: "Glory be to the One, who created in pairs all things that the earth produces, as well as themselves, and other things they do not know." Quran, CH36: V36. The verse conveys several points: bear in mind that Quranic verses were revelations addressed hundreds of years ago, in an era where science wasn't as developed as it is today. On the one hand, the verse could signify that pairs grow from the earth, i.e., plants and species of differentiated sexes. *Human pair* (males and female) is another characterization of the verse. On the other hand, it can allude to dichotomies such as love/hate, bravery/cowardice, extroversion/introversion, light/dark, good/evil, and so on. One facet, condition, or notion and its opposite to bring about balance in life as illustrated by the yin and yang model of existence, order versus chaos. The verse specifically referred to the knowledge of the unknown ("and other things they do not know") as unceasing and that we'll be perpetually seeking it; otherwise there will be no purpose for making ends meet, as we humans thrive on discoveries, findings, and breakthroughs. Having the answer to everything will put a halt to an adventurous future.

* * *

What quantum physics teaches us is that everything
we thought was physical is not physical.

— Bruce H. Lipton

Most religions preach honesty, sincerity, love, and peace — righteous reasoning as explained by almost every culture and society of their time. The time line is imperative as to know when these viewpoints were translated, interpreted, and understood. Religion is a model designed to unveil answers throughout time and a guide to make known what's wrong from right, dark from light, good from evil, and one notion from its counterpart. Accepting both counterparts as part of life and being able to control ourselves is what religion is all about—it's not a tool or weapon that is meant to threaten and instill fear in people. Taking a particular pathway is a matter of choice and will only manifest in what you attract. The idea of good and evil and whether one will lead to heaven and the other to hell is a very controversial subject that will be discussed later in this book. Heaven and hell could be elucidated in many different ways; interestingly, many are fixated on only one interpretation and are so eager to disprove all the others that this is ill-judged. We don't have a sheer understanding of life itself; hence, no one is in a supreme position to interpret what's to transpire in the afterlife. Reality itself is a subject of limitless possibilities and so are interpretations of science and religion. Nothing is black or white.

Let us look at another example of the electron and its counterpart, the positron. When these two come together, energy is generated. The importance of creation in pairs in the universe also gained momentum with the discovery of quarks within the protons and neutrons as well. The fact that the description of scientific phenomena in the Quran could not be accounted for by the knowledge discovered at the time of the Prophet is not the only outstanding point. However, the fact that these phenomena are still not fully recognized or understood means that we haven't yet unlocked every possible interpretation in this book, and so it continues. That's the whole point! Our curiosity becomes even more noteworthy when we examine the scientific data stated in the verses of the Quran that reflect a higher intelligence's omnipotence, art, science, and design. For example, the statement in chapter 21, verse 30 that "the universe was created from an integrated mass, as the raw material of the heavens and the earth were closed up before God split them" could not possibly be the word of a mortal at the time of the Prophet. This proved that a higher power had created matter and the universe and that He had preset objectives in His mind. These facts testify to His miraculous existence and the splendor of His art.

* * *

Conscious Particles

Physicists are made of atoms. A physicist is an attempt by an atom to understand itself.

— Michio Kaku

The double-slit experiment is one of those things that will raise more questions than answering any. There are many lessons to take away nevertheless, so bear with me. Consciousness or observation can impact the material world surrounding us; this is called the Copenhagen interpretation. An example will be used as an illustration of the study conducted (double-slit experiment) to clarify the Copenhagen interpretation even further, but let's lay out the concept first. According to the Copenhagen interpretation, as long as there is no consciousness observing a system (particles, object, planet, sun), then the system will evolve in the quantum world (waves and superpositions). However, when a conscious observer observes the system, the particles stop obeying the laws of quantum mechanics, and instead of being in a state of superpositions, it snaps to one state. In simple terms, the act of observation creates a definite reality. If this is your first time learning about quantum theory, then this probably has not made any sense to you yet, and that's perfectly fine. It still doesn't make sense to the finest physicists in the world. I promise you it gets easier the more you read through, however. The many worlds hypothesis demonstrates this very clearly. Light was the first thing that explained superposition (being in many states at the same time). However, soon after that, electrons, protons, neutrons, and alpha particles (helium) demonstrated superpositions.

The larger a thing is, the harder it is to conduct an experiment that shows superposition. Mostly, it's much easier at a quantum (small) scale, but so far everything seems to be capable of being in a superposition state. So *everything* here includes people as well. Now among the many questions lurking in your mind right now must be *What on earth is a superposition?* Let's have a look at the example below to hammer out this concept.

To understand this example, we need first to understand how particles act. If we randomly shoot a tiny object, say a marble, at a screen, we see a pattern on the screen where it went through the slit and struck, as shown in figure 1.1. Now, if we add a second slit next to the first, we expect to see a second band duplicated next to the first as shown in figure 1.2.

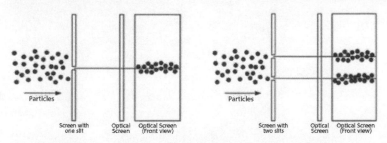

Particles

Screen with one slit | Optical Screen | Optical Screen (Front view)

Particles

Screen with two slits | Optical Screen | Optical Screen (Front view)

[**Figure 1.1.** Big solid marble particles fired through a single slit]
[**Figure 1.2.** Big solid marble particles fired through a double slit]

Now, let's look at light particles (or waves). When the light waves hit the single slit, they radiate out, striking the screen wall with the most intensity, directly aligned with the slit as shown in figure 2.1; this is similar to the line that the marbles make with the single-slit experiment. However, when we add the second slit, something different happens. If one light wave meets another, they cancel each other out. So, now there is an interference sequence on the screen wall. Places where the two tops meet are the highest intensity, hence the bright lines, and where they cancel each other out, there is nothing as illustrated in figures 2.2 and 2.3.

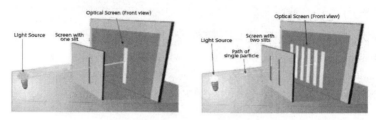

[**Figure 2.1.** Light particles (waves) fired through a single slit]
[**Figure 2.2.** Light particles (waves) fired through a double slit]

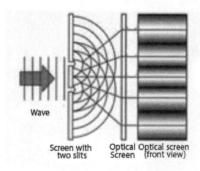

[**Figure 2.3.** Light particles (waves) fired through a double slit]

So that means when we throw things that are matter like the marble particles through two slits, we get the screen results in figure 1.2. Moreover, with light waves, we get the screen results in figure 2.2. Now, let's shrink all the tools to quantum size and redo the experiment using an electron instead of a big marble particle. An electron is very tiny matter, like a small marble. If we fire an electron stream through a one-slit screen, it'll behave just like the big-marble particle, a single band as shown in figure 3.1. If we shoot these tiny electron beams through two slits, we are supposed to get two bands like the big marbles, but we don't! We get an interference pattern (just like waves) as shown in figure 3.2! We fired electrons, which are tiny bits of matter, but we get a pattern on the screen like light waves, not like little marbles! How? How can pieces of matter create an interference pattern like waves? It doesn't make sense. Physicists are smart, of course: they said maybe those balls are bouncing off each other and creating that pattern.

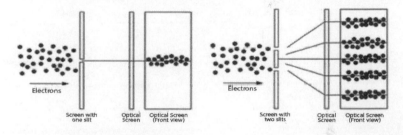

[**Figure 3.1.** Tiny electrons fired through a single slit]
[**Figure 3.2.** Tiny electrons fired through a double slit]

So, they decide to fire electrons through one at a time, as shown in figure 4. There is no way they could bounce off each other right now. However, after an hour of this, the same interference pattern seems to emerge. The conclusion is inescapable: the electron leaves as one particle becomes a wave of potentials, then splits into two particles and goes through both slits and interferes with itself. That is the superposition! The single electron is technically everywhere. Physicists were utterly baffled by this, so they decided to take a peek and see which slit it went through.

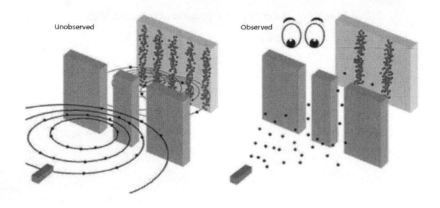

[**Figure 4.** Electrons fired through two slits unobserved (left)
Electrons fired through two slits observed (right)]

They put a measurement device by one slit to see which one it went through and let it fly. However, the quantum world is far more mysterious than they could've imagined. When they observed the electron, it reverted to behaving like a normal marble particle—it produced two bands! It was as if it went back in time and then went through the double slit behaving like a marble, as if it knew it was being observed! The very act of observing or measuring which slit it went through meant it went through one, not both. The electron decided to act differently as if it were aware it was being watched. It was here that physicists stepped forever into the strange never-world of quantum events. What is matter? Particles or waves? Also, waves of what? And what does an observer have to do with any of this? The observer collapsed the wave function simply by observing.

*Quantum physics tells us that nothing that observed
is unaffected by the observer. That statement, from
science, holds enormous and powerful insight.*

It means that every person sees a different truth
because everyone is creating what they see.

— Neale Donald Walsch

* * *

Schrödinger's Cat

Quantum physics thus reveals a basic oneness of the universe.

— Erwin Schrödinger

Schrödinger's cat refers to a theoretical experiment explained by one of the world's foremost physicists, Erwin Schrödinger, who used it to illustrate the weird nature of quantum theory. As we have established with quantum entanglement and the double-slit experiment, we now know that quantum theory dictates that, until a particle is measured and observed, it exists in all the space it could be in simultaneously. So, if there is a probability that a particle could be found in point A at one state and in point B at another state and in point C at another, then the particle will be existing in all of those states at the same time. This is referred to as the particle being in a superposition. When the particle is observed, the superposition collapses, and the particle chooses one state to be in over all of the other states, and this is the state that our measuring instrument will observe. If this is true, then it should apply to bigger objects, since all matter is made up of small particles...but of course, we know that it does not happen like that. We observe bigger objects occupying only one state, so Schrödinger came up with the cat example to provide an analogy of how weird the behavior of quantum particles is as described by the quantum world as if it were to happen to larger visible objects.

In this experiment, a cat is placed in a covered, secured metal box, with a bomb that has a fifty percent chance of exploding and killing the cat. While the box is covered, we have no idea if the cat is dead or alive, and only when we open the box will we know whether the cat lived or not. So, if we think of that like a particle using the superposition principle, we would say that while the box was closed and the cat was not being observed, the cat was both dead and alive for it to be in all the states it could be in. Only when we uncovered the box to observe the cat, that is once we carried out our measurement, did the cat's superposition collapse to be either dead or alive. Common sense tells us that before we uncovered the box, the cat was either dead or alive but not both at the same moment. Our active observing didn't force one outcome over the other, but common sense is not something we can hold on to when studying the quantum world. Countless experiments have proved to us that subatomic particles behave in strange ways that we don't observe in larger matter.

The many worlds hypothesis suggests that anything that can happen does happen, so when Schrödinger's cat was observed, in one universe the cat was found to be dead and in another universe, alive. The theory explained it like this: when the cat was in the covered box, it was in the superposition of being dead or alive. When the box was uncovered, a split in the universe occurred, where in one universe the cat was dead, and in another the cat was alive. The implications of this are mind-boggling; every time there is one or more possible option available for the universe, the universe splits and creates copies where all possible outcomes come true. So, for example, there could be a world where Hitler won World War II, a world where a cure for cancer and AIDS has been discovered, a world so advanced in discoveries and unity, a world where finally humanity has learned the secrets of string theory, a world free of disease, a world filled with more chaos, and maybe even a world where Egypt is the world's superpower! At a quantum level, each person sees a distinctive truth because everyone is creating what they see, so why doesn't this reason apply at the macro level? Why do we all see the moon in the same position and many other things fixed in one place? Could it point to the fact that, on a larger scale, we are one unified consciousness reflecting itself in an eluded sense of separation? If yes, then how can our thoughts modify our reality?

The task is not to see what has never been seen
before, but to think what has never been thought
before about what you see every day.

— Erwin Schrödinger

* * *

Laws of Attraction

We live in a universe that responds to what we believe.

— Henry Corbin

The law of attraction is a law many people fail to understand. Do you know that the law of attraction is always in action, just like the law of gravity? It may be a little bit more complicated in terms of timing and mind-set, but it's similar to any other law that governs the universe. If you let an apple fall, it will always go down, it will never go up; and if you position two magnets facing each other, they will still attract or repel each other. So, like the laws of gravity, magnetism, electromagnetism, or any other force that regulates the universe, the law of attraction is no exception. Gravity is an unseen force, yet it's held as true because of the equations that associate it to reality. If only there were an equation that corresponds to love, hate, and all human emotions, feelings, and thoughts, people would've had a better understanding of how it works. Unfortunately, there is no equation for it yet, and people fail to understand how it works, if at all. Let me remind you that scientists are still struggling to attain the theory of everything. Quantum physics doesn't abide by the gravitational force that we once believed in blindly. Therefore, until this equation is realized, we are in an unfamiliar realm, and according to modern science, gravity is as ambiguous as the law of attraction.

According to string theory, what we know for sure about the human body is that it is made of energy—a vast mass of vibrating energy. Your body is a molecular structure, a mass of energy at a very high speed of vibration. If you look at your body through a microscope, you'll see that energy dancing right before your eyes. Now here's something that will keep you thinking for the rest of your life: when your mind (or consciousness) moves out of your body, the body doesn't stop moving. If you went to a funeral and examined the remains of the body, you'd see it moving. If it weren't moving, how could it ever change to dust? You moved into your body, and you will move out of it; therefore, how you use your mind will dictate the vibration you are in. For the sake of discussion, imagine the mind frame as an imaginary circle. Now, cut this circle in half: one-half is the conscious mind, and the other half is your subconscious mind. The subconscious mind was programmed when you were a baby; this half circle was wide open, and everything that went on around you went right in there. All the energy that went in your half-circle subconscious mind formed something called *paradigm*. Paradigm is information, and it's a multitude of habits; you are a product of your environment, but before that childhood, you were a product of your genetic strain that goes back for generations. That theory was discussed in depth by Sigmund Freud; let's consider this paradigm that you have developed as X-type of energy. Now, you've got the ability on a conscious level—the other half of the circle—to think, and you can think anything you want. As you think, you build ideas: there's a power or force flowing into your consciousness, and it never stops. It flows to and through you, and as it flows in, you will start thinking and will probably think X-type thoughts; therefore, you'll be in an X-type vibration (positive, negative, or anywhere in between on that spectrum), and that will produce X-type results.

* * *

The power of creating a better future is
contained in the present moment. You create a
good future by creating a good present.

— Eckhart Tolle

It is the results you want to change, and to improve the outcomes you have to change what you attract. You see your thoughts on a conscious level control the vibration that you are in on a subconscious level. Vibration is nothing but an idea. It's the law of the universe: everything vibrates, nothing rests. We live in an ocean of motion. The thoughts that you think control the vibration that your body is in and that dictates how you act but also dictates what you attract. You attract energy that is in harmony with you, with your own vibration. You attract people that are in harmony with you; everything operates on frequencies, and there are an infinite number of frequencies, and you usually click with like-minded people on a certain frequency just like a radio station does with its corresponding signal. If that person is not on the same level of frequency in terms of beliefs, hobbies, ideas, interests, background, commonalities, whatever it may be, you won't be in harmony, and the analogous radio signal will be fuzzy and unclear. You won't be comfortable. The more common experiences shared, the more harmony synchronizes in an interaction between you and others—the clearer the signal. So, if you make a conscious effort on where you stand in this sea of frequencies and become more aware of who you are as a person and what you aspire to be and which direction you yearn for, just like a radio frequency, the only music you are going to attract is the music that is tuned into the vibration you are in. Why do we know and believe so much in how radio frequencies and TV signals work but not understand how the same applies to everything else, including human energy?

Now, it's the paradigm that has been controlling this vibration. You can quickly change your thinking, but that doesn't change anything unless you change your paradigm, and if you don't change your paradigm, nothing happens. So, if you keep attracting what you don't want, understand this: it's your paradigm that is causing the problem. You can think a Y-type thought which is different from the X-type paradigm conditioning. It isn't going to go anywhere. When you get emotionally involved with a Y-type thought on a conscious level (the emotional mind usually occurs on the subconscious level), the paradigm in your subconscious level will kick that Y-type thought back out if the paradigm is conditioned to an X-type background. You know why? Because it's very uncomfortable. It's like stepping out of the box and doing things differently, and we don't like doing things differently because it causes much discomfort. It's incredibly vital to understand this because the paradigm and your thoughts do indeed control the vibration you are in, and your vibration is going to dictate what you are going to attract. People in poverty consciousness will continue to attract lack and limitations. It has nothing to do with your educated mind located in your conscious mind, where you can gather all kinds of information. Have you ever wondered why some people have such an educated mind, with advanced degrees like PhDs, but they don't come across like that? Paradigm. Laws of attraction.

You've got to change your vibration and then your whole world will change. Proctor Gallagher talked about how someone introduced Y-type ideas to his X-type paradigm, and it took him over nine years to figure out this concept of changing his paradigm, and when he did, it changed his results automatically. It's because you start attracting something new, something different. That's what everyone wants: we want to reprogram our paradigm into positive ways of thinking and to eliminate the negatives. When you are not feeling well, you are vibrating on a negative frequency. One way to change that is to force yourself to think and make a conscious effort to bring about thoughts of gratitude. Being grateful is the most powerful way to attract positive thoughts. Also, this will manifest itself in something bigger that replicates and divides into something even more significant and will result in more things to be grateful for. If you're angry with someone, try to change how you feel by forcing your paradigm of feeling into pity or forgiveness. If you feel sympathy toward a person who made you angry, this puts you straight in their shoes. Everyone has their own paradigm. This bridges many gaps of understanding among people, and if you want to attract wealth, health, and happiness, consider changing your paradigm.

> *The mind is a powerful instrument. Every*
> *thought, every emotion that you create changes*
> *the very chemistry of your body.*

> — Sadhguru

* * *

How Do We Change a Paradigm?

Changing paradigms can be essential to attracting what you desire in your life. A paradigm by definition is a typical example or pattern of something, a model. So, what a subconscious paradigm is to us is a pattern or programming through constant repetition of thought, expression, belief, or habit. This usually happens during our early years of childhood. A set of beliefs is set in stone, deep in our unconsciousness. We don't even realize it when we grow up. You might be approached by someone telling you that you should start to believe that you can make your annual salary in a month. You might say *Well, that would be nice*, but your paradigm isn't programmed that way and hence will never attract corresponding results until you change your set of beliefs, habits, and thoughts. One way to change that is to make the most out of the subconscious-mind programming process:

1. Focus on one affirmation for some time—at least four weeks.
2. Do it every night before going to sleep or just as you wake up.
3. Get into a routine of it, thereby creating neuronal wiring in the same place and time.
4. Find five to ten minutes during the day to repeat it.

Now, there are so many other ways you can change your paradigm, including changing your mind-set toward something; in particular, a belief, idea, habit, or thought. It's more powerful than you think. Brain reprogramming works for everyone. Realize that there's zero value in negative thoughts. Wanting to diet is one thing, and believing that your eating habits aren't working is another. To reprogram your brain, you have to honestly believe that negative thoughts and habits hold no value to you. Access the subconscious mind through relaxation, meditation, and praying.

1. Move to a quiet room where you won't be disturbed.
2. Take ten deep breaths at a time, each time imagining yourself sinking deeper into the bed, chair, or floor.
3. Once you've reached complete relaxation, begin to visualize your perfect day.

Try to change that mind-set for the sake of experimentation. However, you have to believe in the process. That's how it worked for so many people who genuinely trusted the process. People like Jim Carrey and Matthew McConaughey are two famous figures who affirm this method and explain ever so eloquently how it impacted them—how it indeed changed everything in their lives and made them happier, more prosperous, abundant, and enlightened people. Proctor Gallagher Institute is designed to work with people in this regard. Proctor Gallagher himself states that he was born in a household that made him believe money was scarce and that he should accept what he had. He was happy with what he had but didn't allow it to lead his life. When he grew up, he changed his paradigm by repeating to himself every day and every hour the sentence *I am going to have a large income from multiple sources.* Proctor Gallagher changed his paradigm and thus attracted opportunities that set him on this path of thought. That's precisely what happened with Jim Carrey with the fake five-million-dollar check he kept in his wallet. You need to believe it and set your mind to it, and you'll find yourself in control of your destiny.

CHAPTER 2:
BIRTH OF CONSCIOUSNESS, TRANSCENDENCE, AND NEAR-DEATH EXPERIENCES

The life of this world is only the enjoyment of deception.

— Quran, CH3: V185.

Consciousness and Near Death

Several events in my life revealed powerful cues that led to an intuitively better understanding of consciousness. Many believe that consciousness lies in your brain's neural system while others believe it to be a spirit that drives your body like a car's engine. It's fascinating how one can assert their own beliefs on others then refuse to accept any other concept beyond their boundary of knowledge. We also translate meanings that could go in any direction and twist them to favor our views. Now, here is what we should all extract from what we have discovered through science: anything can be, and the truth is that *we* shape our realities. Whatever I merely explain next is what I gathered and attracted that formed *my* reality. All the signs, serendipities, facts, theories, and circumstances that I've been through led me to my truth, and my truth doesn't necessarily have to be yours! We are all exposed to unique experiences that define our lives in ways that leave no room for absolute truths to be imposed on everyone. My reality will most certainly be different from yours, so what's important is to clear your mind and listen—to listen in a way that extends your understanding of what's different from you and to bridge the gap among everyone and against all odds, finding a way to coexist as a unified species. Only then will we be able to reach one truth that ultimately lies within us. That's how humanity started before the great divide. If you listen to your heart, it will surely take you to the answers that you are looking for; silence will attract the responses to you. Silence in its absolute form is the absence of thoughts and noise created by the mind to develop any division, hate, or anger toward the other. What's crucial to understand here is that time is not a factor, so don't let it hinder your trust in the process. Time is just a construct our mind creates. The answers may come to you within days, weeks, months, or even years, but they will come to you when they do. The more you believe in that and believe in yourself, the more likely it will happen.

To put things into perspective, the difference between successful people and those who fail is that the successful ones believe so immensely not just in themselves but also in the fact that they will succeed no matter how many times they fail. Those who fail stop believing they will succeed and stop trying. Failure is guaranteed in that case. Plant the seed of belief by writing it on a piece of paper and place it in your wallet or purse; leave it there and never stop believing it will happen! It'll sprout when it's time to grow. Each species has its life cycle, span, and rate of growth. Let life take its course the same way it's doing with everything in existence.

* * *

Treasure the magnificent being that you are and recognize first and foremost you're not here as a human being only. You're a spiritual being having a human experience.

— Wayne Dyer

Practically, all matter is energy condensed to a slow vibration. We are all one unified consciousness experiencing itself subjectively. There is no such thing as the death of a soul; life is a dream, an illusion, and we're the imagination of ourselves. If everything in existence is in the form of energy vibrating in different frequencies, then what separates living organisms from inanimate objects? It's consciousness. And what is consciousness? Is it neural signals in our brains? Can it be replicated or created then possibly planted in robots or AI? That's a whole new topic that I will explore later—the rise of artificial intelligence versus divine intelligence and the fate of the human race, and whether it is at an impasse we may never predict or science will lead us right to it. I believe we need to fully comprehend our own consciousness before we start challenging it with further qualms.

Biocentrism (another theory of everything) is a theory proposed by an American scientist back in 2007 that I find intriguing. It suggests that life is the heart of reality and the universe. It explains that life is the core of everything and that it sprouted to create the universe, not the other way around. The theory builds on quantum physics by adding the element of life to the equation. Biology is in a race with physics now to solve the universe's most profound mystery.

* * *

What the caterpillar calls the end, the
rest of the world calls a butterfly.

— Richard Bach

Now let's tap into biology and take a closer look at near-death experiences and studies that predict bizarre possibilities. Near-death experiences (NDE)—to those who have experienced them—display a clear understanding that life doesn't stop when you die. You get access to a realm with no account of space or time. Dr. Eben Alexander, an American Harvard-graduate neurosurgeon, did not believe in heaven or hell until he experienced an NDE episode himself. He underwent an out-of-body experience in 2008 after suffering an immense seizure, and he lapsed into a coma that lasted seven days. His brain was arrested by a rare attack of meningitis, and he related his experience during the coma: "Those who have had near-death experiences will tell you that realm is far more real than this world, more crisp, vibrant, alive. So, I was communicating directly with God? Absolutely. Expressed this way, it sounds grandiose. But when it's happening, it didn't feel this way. Instead, I felt like I was doing what every soul is able to do when they leave their bodies." In 2012, he published a book called *Proof of Heaven: A Neurosurgeon's Journey into the Afterlife.* This book highlights that science can determine that the brain does not create consciousness and that consciousness continues into an afterlife by surviving bodily death. Dr.

Alexander recounts being in a dark landscape of primordial ooze, then gradually ascending toward a higher world of color, light, and celestial music. Lifted by butterfly wings, he encounters an angelic young woman and finally finds himself in the presence of a divine being that he calls *om* for the sound he hears in his presence. His personal experience as a neurosurgeon allowed him to express his journey scientifically but at the same time prove that consciousness is independent of the brain and that death is a transitional phase into another realm that we do not know about. He published another book called *The Map of Heaven: How Science, Religion, and Ordinary People Are Proving the Afterlife*, reiterating the existence of an afterlife and that the brain is indeed separate from our consciousness. In 2017, his third book, *Living in a Mindful Universe: A Neurosurgeon's Journey into the Heart of Consciousness*, explained the higher purpose of consciousness backed up by scientific findings and discussed spiritual realms and how they lead to a profound understanding of a peaceful world.

Dr. Alexander received lots of criticism, especially from Sam Harris who claimed in his blog that his books were "alarmingly unscientific" and that he couldn't prove any of his experience in a logical fashion. This could be true. However, Dr. Alexander is not the only one to experience an out-of-body or near-death experience. According to numerous studies, many people have reported the same kinds of experiences, and when they regained consciousness, they recalled the same details of heaven and hell. Moreover, at first they were floating in the room looking down at their own body, observing every small element in the room and listening to the conversations taking place, but in reality they were clinically dead. They were technically unconscious, so how could they hear or see such things with such detail? And furthermore, how does one explain quantum particles "scientifically"?

Have you heard of the woman who gave birth three months after she was pronounced dead, or of another who was still alive when she was placed into a body bag in the morgue? Why do these dreadful stories happen? The reason is the absence of universal guidelines for doctors when it comes to pronouncing a person dead. Even among doctors, the boundary of death isn't thoroughly agreed on. You're dead only when a doctor declares you dead. A person declared dead when their heart stops can be revived in many instances. In 2013, a study revealed that in some cases where CPR was applied for at least thirty-eight minutes, a person could still be restored thereafter with no lasting brain damage. As soon as the brain stem permanently ceases to function, there's no way to reverse it. Even if a ventilator is employed, if the brain stem stops, the person's heart will eventually stop beating. The most critical fact about the brain is this: it bequeaths to us the one thing that makes us human, our consciousness. The irreversible loss of consciousness is the definition of death. It is for this particular reason that doctors should declare a patient dead, when the functional state of the brain stem is halted. The Quran points out that sleep is like death and death like sleep. "It is He [God], Who takes your souls by night [when you are asleep], and has knowledge of all that you have done by day, then He raises [wakes] you up again that a term appointed [your life period] be fulfilled, then in the end unto Him will be your return. Then He will inform you of what you used to do." Quran, CH6: V60. Also, CH39: V42 states "Allah [God] takes the souls at the time of their death, and that which has not died, in its sleep; He withholds that against which

He has decreed death, but looses the other till a stated term. Surely in that are signs for people who think deeply."

The accurate representation for death is, specifically, when the brain stem no longer functions. It has nothing to do with the function of the heart or whether the person can breathe or not. That primarily accounts for millions of people around the world who have been pronounced dead when, in fact, they were not. Extreme measures should be considered to keep people alive and not proclaim them dead because their heart, breathing, or other bodily functions have stopped. During sleep, the brain-stem effector neurons at some point stop working for a short period, but then we wake up. In 2008, Robert McCarley and Christopher Sinton in Scholarpedia discovered that, during sleep, the effector neurons in the brain stem become hyperpolarized and have almost no action potentials. It's for this reason that most death cases happen during sleep. We should pray that our brain-stem neurons are depolarized so that we may wake up once more and enjoy a new day!

Dr. Mohamed Elshazly, MD, a cardiologist and cofounder of Ember Medical Inc., obtained his degree from Weill Cornell Medicine-Qatar. Subsequently, he moved to the USA and completed his residency in internal medicine at Johns Hopkins Hospital and his fellowship in cardiology and cardiac electrophysiology at Cleveland Clinic. He's currently an assistant professor of medicine at Weill Cornell Medicine. Dr. Elshazly wants to revolutionize medical-emergency response using crowdsourcing technologies to save lives and reduce health-care costs. As a biotech entrepreneur, he's particularly interested in solving health-care issues in a patient centric manner.

"Biotech solutions that consider the complexity of health consumer behaviors and needs are the key to creating an alternative and bright future for health care," Dr. Elshazly has stated. Many cardiologists like him work in cardiac intensive care units and take care of critically ill patients who are between life and death, such as sudden cardiac-arrest patients. He is also regularly involved in discussions related to the prognosis of brain-dead patients and how to pronounce patients dead. Dr. Elshazly asserts, "As a doctor, witnessing the sacred moments of human birth and death is a captivating experience that completely shakes you at the core. You witness how human consciousness begins and how it ends. Beyond the initial mesmerizing emotions of observing such experiences, a false sense of arrogance develops over time as we constantly practice detaching ourselves emotionally. We lose on many opportunities to reflect on the meaning of life and the complexity of consciousness until we encounter this one patient, or family, that brings us back to earth from the false status of God. Whether it's a comatose patient who wakes up after many years of hopelessness or a family instilling hope in their loved one with an incurable terminal illness, there are many lessons to be learned. The most important is to be humble, respect the sacredness of life and death experiences and ultimately transcend beyond our prison of beliefs."

Many of us have the right to be skeptical about the truth or reality, and it's understandable because NDE doesn't happen to everyone. So, who does it occur to? And why? More importantly, how does it happen? Let's look at the scientific facts behind a near-death experience. In an NDE, the brain produces a chemical called Dimethyltryptamine (DMT) in minimal quantities. DMT is a naturally occurring chemical found not only in animals but in plants. It's an active hallucinogenic compound found in many plants. Many of these plants (such as water lilies) were used by the ancient Egyptians, and some are used today by tribes that practice spiritual rituals. One of the most common DMT plants is called Ayahuasca. It's called the *spirit medicine* by the indigenous people in the Amazon for its powerful but short-lasting hallucinogenic effect, which is considered one of the most intense psychedelic experiences to be had. There is much resemblance between the Ayahuasca experience and a near-death experience. For those lucky enough—or unlucky for that matter—to have not experienced an NDE before, they can intentionally replicate the process by consuming that psychedelic brew.

* * *

Heal beyond the Prison of Beliefs

*Change is not only inevitable, but always happening.
When you truly embrace this concept of change being
constant, the only thing left to do is grow, detach,
venture inwards, touch the spirit and find your
source, the one responsible for keeping you grounded
through the ever-changing seasons of life.*

— Julie Weiland

The devil's greatest trick is making you believe that he doesn't exist. It's no surprise that life follows the events written in the holy books, for they are predictable, and the cycles of life are also anticipated. Many people know more than we could wish to know about the reality we live in—as the events that take place follow the book to the word. We buy into different aspects of the same system, be it through science, religion, nature, or history. Money was never the answer and is fast becoming the downfall of this planet's ecosystem for the sake of profit. Do we know that we have enough resources and food to be able to achieve ample fulfillment in life if we worked hand-in-hand for it? Regrettably, the entire system is planned to keep us from discovering veracity. Businesses are shaped on secrecy, and without it, the current system could not sustain itself.

The evolution of free energy is adding pressure to the current system. The top CEOs of the world are committing suicide, and we are doing nothing to stop those tragedies, as we've been programmed to act by fear-dependent governments which relentlessly roll out an avalanche of fear each day in forms of audio, visuals, and energy in the air. I believe that some people in high power have made deals with the devil, if they're not the manifestation of the devil himself. No wonder the people controlling the world are of pure evil and no one can do anything about it. Any living soul who is even slightly spiritual will deduce that fear in its distinct, dominant form is enough to confine you from encountering almost all things spiritual or scientific. The real human deficiency here is lack of humane experience, knowledge, and spirituality. The universe is a spiritual conscious thing, and we mirror the universe. We must align or be forgotten. Understanding is easy if you can question what you believe to be your knowledge and beliefs and have the courage to create new ones that serve humanity and the planet as a whole. Only then can we truly experience our magnificent potentials that lay dormant and repressed by hundreds of years–old teachings invented to do just that: control the majority for the gain of the minority.

It's beautiful when you look at the world now from a different perspective, from the standpoint of a spiritual being, not bound by flesh and bones. The more you believe in that, the higher you'll go and the faster you'll reach your ultimate purpose. On the way to achieving this purpose, you'll be provided with tools, dreams, and other supernatural signs that will lead you to your new essence. In this journey, you'll experience bizarre things, and no one will give that to you! You will soon see and feel things beyond human nature. You will become the best version of yourself!

* * *

Ayahuasca and DMT: The Spirit Molecule

Spiritual realization is the core element in the Ayahuasca experience. Ayahuasca is a medicine. Complete purification and cleansing of body, mind, and spirit! In the ceremony, Ayahuasca can initiate a lifelong process of rebirth and transformation. The process requires long-term personal commitment, integrity, compassion, and courage. It is not an easy path, but it can be highly beneficial for those who undertake it with sincerity, determination, and an open heart.

— O. Blanco

After years of research following what initially ignited my fire— Graham Hancock's TEDx talk on The War on Consciousness—I finally decided I was ready for it. Ayahuasca is considered a spiritual plant medicine that heals mentally, physically and spiritually. I was on a phone call with a consultant in a well-known medically licensed center supervising Ayahuasca ceremonies, in Cusco, Peru, when she asked, "Why do you want to book with us?" I paused for a second and told her, "I am following many signs, dreams, and callings for self-discovery, spiritual enlightenment, and most importantly, a pursuit of truth and ego suppression." Then I asked, "How effective is this plant medicine?" She replied, "One hundred percent of our clients report that they have been cured or have found whatever they came here looking for. Most of our clients prior to retreat suffered from depression, obsessive-compulsive disorder (OCD), anxiety, addictions, insomnia and sleep disorders. Some simply came here for spiritual enlightenment and healing. So far, no one left our center reporting anything other than pure bliss, love, understanding, and the human capacity to change miraculously in a short period. It's as if the hands of God have touched their soul." She continued, "But first, you have to make sure you prepare mentally and physically for the experience. That includes changing your diet two weeks before the retreat, not engaging in any sexual activity to prevent energy imbalances, and avoiding medications, recreational drugs, coffee, chocolate or any sugary food, salt, oils, red meat, pork, smoking, and alcohol. These things can have a negative impact and hinder your experience as they don't react well with the brew for reasons that include but are not limited to interference with your state of consciousness and energy levels. You must also develop a high level of respect for the plant."

A sudden realization hit me. If these things don't react well with a plant medicine that is supposed to nourish your body mentally, physically, and spiritually, then what exactly do these things do to your body and in what way do they alter your consciousness and mind? I didn't waste time in suspending all these things; I decided to heed her recommendations straightaway. I developed somewhat of an obsession about the matter and gave it my total, undivided attention. I was so determined to go through the preparation journey with the utmost respect. I refrained from doing anything that could harm my body, made sure I exercised regularly, meditated and prayed more often, and ate vegan, or vegetarian with some fish now and then. I bought the book *DMT: A Spirit Molecule* by Dr. Rick Strassman, the first physician who began experimenting with DMT on volunteers back in the '90s to study its effect on people. I also started watching Joe Rogan's audiovisual podcasts on DMT, which were tremendously insightful (and funny). In my opinion, he is the best person to explain the experience through various interviews. It's not easy to convey what it feels like or what you'll witness. The worst thing that can happen with DMT is experiencing a negative infernal journey, and the second worst is to have to explain what you went through.

* * *

Health is a state of complete harmony of the body, mind
and spirit. When one is free from physical disabilities
and mental distractions, the gates of the soul open.

— B. K. S. Iyengar

My life revolved around this now, resolved to seeking the best version of myself. One of the main reasons I started the purging process was a strong force within me possessing an urge to cleanse and nurture my soul. Long before the experience, I also learned that the Ayahuasca detoxification process could be harrowing and, in rare cases, turn into psychotic breaks. Purging accumulated toxins from my physical body was not a procedure I wanted to go through with dis-ease, so this was a powerful motivation for me to embark on this. I've learned so many things already about the visuals people talk about, the sacred geometry, patterns, Fibonacci's sequence, and how all of this relates to the sacred Islamic geometry, "Subjects saw all sorts of imaginable and unimaginable things. The least complex were kaleidoscopic geometric patterns, which sometimes partook Mayan, Islamic or Aztec qualities." Dr. Rick Strassman. Many people testified how beautiful the geometrical shapes were in their experience: they signified unity, infinite beauty, boundless love, immeasurable order, proportional sequence, and perfection. In Islamic belief, the sacred shapes and patterns hold the same connotation, and in the center of every pattern is the wholeness of the Quran and the unity of consciousness in an infinite pattern. In sacred Islamic art, it's about how the divine wishes itself to be known through human participation. That's why you don't find human signatures on these patterns; it's not about the individual; it's beyond the artist. The patterns are there to promote the universal principals in terms of the structure of nature and the nature of the universe as expressed in arts and crafts. The concept of full, prominent beauty at the center of these shapes and patterns shines through the transient world. Islamic art has three principal forms. The most important is calligraphy, with the words of God that are closest to the revelation. The next is the arabesque, a decorative element. Finally, the foundation is geometry, the knowledge of the eternally existent, in the sense that a hexagon would be a hexagon in a million years, and time wouldn't change that. Within the Quran there is a frontal masterpiece: it's a geometric pattern of a central star and the other stars are cropped. The central star is the Quran, and the reason for cropping the other stars and not having them complete is to describe that pattern as infinite and ever-repeating, indicating that what you're about to enter is the center of the universe. Islamic patterns are symbolic for the central doctrine, which is *Tawheed*, translated as *unity*. The growing patterns themselves are symbolic of the principal aspect of the worshiping term *Thekr* or *remembrance*. These patterns refer to the cosmological aspect of design, the divine plan.

Moreover, the remembrance and the repetition of it is like continually remembering that all is one, and we are all one. If that's how Islam explains the patterns, geometry, the infinite growth of the shapes, and the divine order they manifest as, how is it that these are the very same visuals experienced by the consumption of DMT? What is mind-blowing is that our own body produces the chemical composition of DMT in the pineal gland of the brain, and it's induced the minute you become an embryo; hence, in many traditions and religions, abortion after almost forty-five days is considered a sin only because, when DMT is produced in an embryo (that's approximately the same time the gender of the baby is determined), it's considered the birth of a spirit.

There are two main chemical families in the psychedelic drugs: the phenethylamines and tryptamine. The best-known phenethylamine is mescaline, which is derived naturally from the American-southwest cactus but has been pharmaceutically converted to what we know as MDMA and ecstasy. Tryptamine, however, is a derivative of an amino acid present in our diet; serotonin is also a tryptamine. DMT is a tryptamine as well and is the simplest psychedelic. It has antiaddictive properties. Psilocybin, the active ingredient for so-called magic mushrooms, is a well-known tryptamine too. DMT and magic mushrooms are usually ingested in their natural forms and therefore have a different impact on us, making them much safer than MDMA and ecstasy. DMT is present in our bodies and will always test positive. However, it isn't activated until we add a monoamine oxidase inhibitor (MAOI). A common ingredient in Ayahuasca is the shrub psychotria viridian (also known as chacruna), which contains the psychoactive compound DMT, but without mixing it with an MAOI, it won't produce an effect.

Not only is Ayahuasca a Pineal Gland activator and stimulator, but Ayahuasca is also a powerful Pineal Gland Developer. Clinical researcher, Maps Dotorg. Moreover, Ayahuasca puts our seven chakras in order (which many religions recommend, but religious institutions disregard), and Ayahuasca unlocks the right side of the brain, as well as the frontal lobes of the brain, a scientifically proven fact by Dr. Rick Strassman. Also called the Vine of the Soul, it is sacred and a natural psychotropic. The Amazonian term *Ayahuasca* means the freeing of the spirit or the pure essence of the soul. To consume it is to be purged and cleansed. It purifies the physical, mental, emotional states, and the spiritual body, and it reaches deep within and removes the layers of debris relating to our years-old fears and illusions which cast a shadow over the soul. It's an ego-killer and removes from us all harmful matter correlated with dark energies. Additionally, Ayahuasca helps to retrieve and reconnect with ancient knowledge and wisdom embedded in our very DNA and psyche and to journey into the past, present, and future, including other realms, dimensions, and parallel universes.

The plant indeed has a spirit, and in the eye of a shaman, it is an influential physician and medicine. Through the application of this master teacher, one can access the unknown, intangible realm inhabited by other beings, trigger dreams and visions and the liberation of all matter. Living in a culture fearful of the use of mind-altering substances—what we call *drugs* in the Western world—natural plants and medicines are sometimes regarded as a hazardous and superficial form of spirituality. The opposite is true, Dr. Rick Strassman states in *DMT: The Spirit Molecule*: "I was neither intellectually nor emotionally prepared for the frequency with which contact with beings occurred in our studies, nor the often utterly bizarre nature of these experiences. Also surprising were the common themes of what these beings were doing with so many of our volunteers: manipulating, communicating, showing, helping, questioning. It was definitely a two-way street." He also added about one of his volunteers: "The most reassuring experience of my life, the separation of his mind and body was effortless, and he decided that 'if death is like this, there's nothing to worry about.'"

The service involved with the master teacher accelerates an awakening of our multidimensional self and our interconnection. It sanctions a glimpse beyond the illusion of what we perceive to be a reality through to a deeper connection with our planet and the higher realms, by channeling intensely heartfelt insights, profound messages, and discerning visions for a comprehensive apprehension of the truth and magic of life and inner self. Shamanic traditions have utilized Ayahuasca and other medicinal plants to summon far-reaching mystical experiences, refines in consciousness, and as curing agents for thousands of years. Their telepathic powers are associated with supernatural forces inhabiting their tissues, and they were divine gifts to the earliest human beings on Earth. It's speculated that ancient Egyptians used a similar plant containing DMT to gain the knowledge and insights about astrology, the afterlife, math, art, medicine, and construction of the great pyramids. It could've been the root cause of ancient religions in the first place.

A spiritual experience lies at the core of the Ayahuasca plant. Purification of a clouded mind and body and of an obscured soul in a healing ceremony can facilitate a profound process of spiritual awakening and maturation. This process of development and spiritual growth can continue even if Ayahuasca is not taken again. The experience is decidedly unique to each person as it enables a direct connection with the deepest parts of the subconscious mind, enhancing a deep relationship with our true higher self and deep inner soul.

Ayahuasca bestows a window into our soul and shows us who we really are and who we can become. We firmly believe that the perks gained from learning about Ayahuasca are incalculable, both from a personal and planetary standpoint. There is no plant or medicine on the planet as esteemed, prominent, influential, or respected as Ayahuasca. Furthermore, the Western world is slowly starting to acknowledge this plant phenomenon, with an ever-increasing number of people, CEOs, neurologists, academics, scientists, philosophers, believers, and nonbelievers heading toward South America to experience Ayahuasca. In DMT The Spirit molecule Dr. Rick Strassman states, "Ironically, we may have to rely more upon science, especially freewheeling fields of cosmology and theoretical physics, than our conservative religious traditions for satisfactory models and explanations of these 'Spirit-world' experiences."

The medicine Ayahuasca—also known as The Queen of the Forest and believed to be the most potent of the teacher plants—is consumed in a traditional ceremonial setting under the guidance of a shaman (a master trained in the use of the vine) or *Ayahuasquero*. It is crucial to have an experienced shaman present to administer the ceremony, a person who has a deep understanding of the forces in action and how to maintain the energies in balance. Ayahuasca is a formidable purgative that allows extensive and exhaustive cleansing through vomiting and diarrhea, and is a natural antibiotic, robust painkiller, vigorous disinfectant, and it speeds the healing of wounds. For some individuals, the weight felt in their life is the heaviness of past emotional experiences. Ayahuasca can aid in surfacing memories to be confronted, addressed, and set free through purging. The purging aspect of the Ayahuasca experience is tremendously beneficial as it also liberates the body from impurities that sap our energy. This deep-cleansing process is natural detoxification, which regenerates physical vitality, sparkle, harmony, and glow. It is through our purge that we make new space for higher energy, clarity, positivity, creativity, and vibrancy to enter into our life.

The indigenous people of South America consider Ayahuasca as a teacher, capable of transferring the drinker to other dimensions of space and time, where past, present, and future are all equally accessible, both one's own life path and those of others.

Everyone's journey with it is unique and personal. The plant-teacher guides us to the deepest components of our subconscious where, with our conscious self, we can come face-to-face and then understand and dispose of deep-rooted emotional traumas and behavioral habits that are hindering our lives and stopping us from being our authentic selves. Negative behavioral patterns, bad habits, diseases, and egoistic tendencies can be intimately analyzed to figure out their origin and nature.

It is common to experience a regression back to the circumstance or source of a problem by reliving the trauma. To relive that past experience is to gain new insights and well-rounded understanding, allowing resolution or closure. Dreamlike episodes, where personal messages from spirits are obtained, cause the ceremony participant to reevaluate their life with a much deeper understanding of why they are living, what their purpose is, and what is needed to fulfill that purpose. People ingesting it often report significant changes in the way they perceive life and how they feel about themselves, and most of the time, they experience a growing sense of direction, purpose, inner strength, creativity, wisdom, and power. "People who take it report that they're blasted out of their body, like out of a canon, then they go out 'somewhere' and encounter beings of various sorts, then ten minutes later they're back. Virtually everyone reports that, which is really strange," states Dr. Jordan Peterson, a Canadian clinical psychologist and a professor of psychology at the University of Toronto. "If you give people Psilocybin and they have a mystical experience, which is very common among people who take these sorts of chemicals, then their personality transforms permanently, such that one year later they're one standard deviation higher in openness, and openness is the creativity dimension. It seems to be a permanent transformation. So that's really remarkable. About eighty percent of the people who undergo the Johns Hopkins experiments report that the experience is like one of the three most important things that's ever happened to them."

Not everyone approaches this medicine with the same requirements. The magic of Ayahuasca lies in its ability to figure out, focus, diagnose, heal, and transcend one's limitations, conditioning, cultural programming, negative thoughts, and fears. It takes us to a genuine foundational area within each of us that instinctively and suddenly recognizes the answer that wants us to achieve what we desire in life and to be true to ourselves. It shows us how to trust this new inner voice that was once ignored and to achieve a more fulfilling lifestyle. The underlying work of the shaman is the comprehension that nature is alive, is conscious, and has intelligence; that plants have spirits who can assist us to heal as humans; that an answer to any disease can be found in nature. It is viable for one to see and communicate with these spirits during an Ayahuasca experience. For instance, one can contact these plant spirits to learn their medicinal functions and how to collect and prepare them for healing uses.

Ayahuasca enables the integration of the self with our higher self; this integration transpires the true self. The completely active brain shreds the fear-based, ego-mind troubles that infect the human state. The light of our higher consciousness presents the mask of our pretentious self as irrelevant. It ceases to be of significance in impressing anyone by being right or ultimately better than others or to be generally ashamed of who we are. A radiant, joyous, light, and playful sense embraces our being, and we become resolved in our humanity and our divinity. We stop thinking and start knowing. In this grand time of human awakening, when more people search for higher guidance and authentic direction in their lives, the sacred medicine takes them on the path that leads to the remembrance of one's honest and true self. Ayahuasca delivers the most direct and immediate pathway to self-inquiry, and one only has to grab the opportunity that it offers for boundless personal and spiritual development!

It is one of the most efficient confrontational processes of healing one's inner self, and in participating one is moved beyond the muddled and noisy mind into the natural heart center, where peace and unbounded love reside. Furthermore, as with the microcosm of a single human soul that reflects the universe at large, humanity now finds itself seeking the remembrance of its true nature.

* * *

When the earth is shaken with its mighty shaking, and when the earth brings forth its burdens, and the human asks: "What is the matter with it?" On that Day it shall proclaim its news, for your Lord will have revealed to it. On that Day mankind shall issue in scatterings to see their deeds. Whosoever has done an atom's weight of good shall see it, and whosoever has done an atom's weight of evil shall see it.

— *Quran, CH99: V30.*

Ayahuasca will without any reservations or pretense show your most deeply buried details of yourself. Inspect them for a reevaluation and reintegration, for this is the only mechanism to spiritual development. Not one aspect of the shadow self shall be left behind, be swept under the carpet, or remain unforgiven. It will present your worst self and most negative aspects of your personality and reveal to you how to fully heal yourself. It will tell you no lies, and will with total and utter clarity illustrate your effect on others and what you need to adapt and what hardships you need to let go of. Ayahuasca, in all her wisdom, unveils your most immediate troubles and grants you a higher and better perspective on them, one that cannot be acquired by the everyday rational mind. It shows your pains and fears so that you might climb the ladder of personal growth ever so high by relearning the concept of unconditional love—the remembrance of your true essence and, certainly, the essence of all that is. Make no mistake about it, this is no walk in the park; this is serious labor on the self that requires paramount commitment, conscientiousness, and thorough, disciplined preparation. Evading issues prior to the workshop such as proper diet will only reduce the effect and point the outcome of the whole exercise toward failure.

Our mainstream society finances and promotes so many unhealthy temptations that go against our well-being, that aspect is challenged rigorously; this is one of the prerequisites to proper preparation, and eventually, true to form, I found myself requiring much less food than normally. This is the hard proof that spiritual work has immediate real-world results.

Every soul has a journey and a story. It is thus up to every person to determine how they will get from one point to the other. After all, every journey is just as significant and just as beautiful. Hence, I heartily recommend these sessions to all because ultimately everyone is on a journey of self-exploration. The companionship of shamans who will support you is one of warmth and love. Their beautiful chants carry you peacefully and providently through your darkest hours, your most exhilarating visions, and your most profound lessons.

However—and I say this without exaggeration—the group of beautiful people embarking on the same journey as you will be your greatest teachers while you are there. Furthermore, if you have never honestly felt connected to another person on a soul level, expect that to arise with the entire group as you are shown the illusion of separation and the truth of universal love. If I could sum up this incredible journey with the sacred medicinal plants of Peru, I would say this: those who have not experienced fundamental knowing, who have not been embraced by direct spiritual experience, they know nothing yet. This is your chance to understand the infinity that resides beyond the mind, to remember and honor who you truly are.

Participants who encounter the Ayahuasca experience report having profound spiritual revelations regarding their purpose in life, the true essence of the universe, as well as deep insights as to how to be the best version of themselves they can possibly be. It is almost always said that people experience intense positive changes in their life after consuming Ayahuasca. It is also often reported that individuals experience gaining access to so-called spiritual dimensions and making contact with various sovereign entities that serve to function as guides or healers.

Ayahuasca focuses and aligns the person with the ancient nature of spirituality. It resets our biological clock according to the universal understanding of time and harmonizes our natural brain chemistry. The corresponding shift in our values, priorities, and self-image produces a constant rebirth, a transformational beginning. This quality is the most life-changing gift, and the one most craved by many seekers. People experiencing Ayahuasca ceremonies particularly attain considerable mental, psychological, and spiritual progress, comparable to that accomplished through intensive decades of psychotherapy, and often in a remarkably short time.

Studies exploring Ayahuasca's history and uses often fail to explain the remarkably transformational processes it establishes. Its numerous effects advance through cathartic, abreactive, and spiritual stages. Experience of universal time is an essential element in this process. Each lesson carries one beyond the previous ones, with revelations according to the character, quality, depth of prior experiences, and the person's stage of consciousness and awareness.

The first effect one notices after ingesting Ayahuasca is a distinctive shift in sensory modality. The tactile and auditory sensitivity enhances, and mental processes and emotions become more intense. At this point, the journey may head into many dimensions. Then soul flight causes a sense of floating and disconnection as one enters other dimensions of hyperspace. The consistency of its effects is indescribable. The spiritual core of consciousness switched on by Ayahuasca cannot be programmed or controlled, though the journey can be guided and swayed by competent shamans. The pharmacological functions of the psychoactive molecule in interaction with the ancient spirits are not enough to define the impact on the psyche. Ayahuasca always interacts with the psychoemotional and spiritual set of each person and the construct of the setting in which it is taken.

*　　*　　*

Words reduce reality to something the human
mind can grasp, which isn't very much.

— Eckhart Tolle

Here I will describe and categorize the effects that the Ayahuasca brew has to offer as precisely as I can, even though words will not do it much justice.

The body under the influence of Ayahuasca can be described as having a pleasurable, tender, friendly, compassionate, warm, and all-encompassing glow. It is manifested intermittently at various unpredictable stages during the experience, but for some, it maintains a constant presence that steadily increases from the beginning and eventually reaches a peak.

Ayahuasca is described by many as extraordinarily sober and clear-headed in its approach when compared to other commonly used psychedelics, such as LSD or psilocybin. It contains a large number of common and unique cognitive effects, although I don't always consider Ayahuasca or DMT as psychedelics even if they are classified as such. The most prominent of these quintessential effects include introspection, acceleration of the thought process, enhancement of the current state of mind, eradication of cultural filters, intriguing feelings of fascination and awe, conceptual thinking, vocabulary suppressions, ego suppression, loss or death, time distortion or collapse, and déjà vu. Many volunteers in Dr. Strassman's experiments reported that their ego and identity were shattered and broken into a million bits and pieces, and they couldn't recognize themselves as separate from the conscious universe anymore. Many experienced a being of some sort sucking their spirit at the speed of light into this tunnel and into space. "This thing sucked me out of my head into outer space. It was clearly outer space, a black sky with millions of stars. I was in a very large waiting room, or something. It was very long. I felt observed. I was taken into space and looked at." A volunteer in Rick Strassman's experiment.

Alongside the stereotypical cognitive effects listed above, Ayahuasca generates certain states that are supposedly rare within all other psychedelics, in a consistent, compelling way. These commonly reported and unique cognitive effects involve: strong and consistent mindfulness (this term is used within psychological texts to refer to states which are actualized through the act of practicing meditation); a sense of focus which characterizes the present moment with stillness; the absence of movement or sound; and clarity of mind. Inspired mindfulness can occur within any psychedelic experience but is unique within Ayahuasca due to how consistently it is manifested and how it can self-sustain itself for days, weeks, months, or even years following a single high dose.

This is an extremely beneficial and therapeutic impact on personal psychological health. On the contrary, other more commonly used psychedelics, such as LSD and psilocybin, tend to induce this effect in a merely casual and temporary form. Ayahuasca induces a state of unity and connectedness, a unique effect because of how consistently it is manifested as an accompanying guide, and because it occasionally leads to ego death or suppression. Other psychedelics such as LSD and psilocybin rarely induce this effect. It establishes a consistent communication with the subconscious, which can be briefly described as a literal communication with an internal voice which alleges to be the subconscious. At lower levels, this is carried out by the subconscious conversing with you through your stream of thought. At higher dosages, however, it becomes a completely audible voice which is capable of lucid and logical conversation at the same level as the ego, and which is arguably self-aware in its own right. Ayahuasca can trigger sustained dream potentiation; regular or occasional use commonly leads to extremely vivid, lucid, and easily remembered dreams in the days and weeks after the experience.

The general cognitive positivity or negativity of an Ayahuasca experience in psychologically balanced individuals depends considerably on how nauseating or purgative the chosen program of preparation is. For instance, paranoia, anxiety, madness, and a difficulty intertwining thoughts together often instantly manifest themselves during uncomfortable conditions of nausea for the inexperienced but remain absent when the user has become accustomed to the purge itself.

It also produces a full range of possible visual enhancements which generally includes sharpened visuals, improved colors, enhanced pattern identification, and visible meandering (melting, breathing, bending, warping, and flowing). In comparison to other psychedelics, this effect can be explained as highly detailed, slow and smooth in motion, and static in their appearance. Users also visualize tracers, after-images, texture and pattern repetition, color shifting, scenery slicing, and sacred geometry. The visible geometry that is present throughout this experience can be explained as perfectly structured in its arrangement, organic in geometric elegance, delicate in complexity, vast in size, rapid and smooth in motion, glossy in color, colorful in design, equal in the number of blurred and sharp edges and in rounded and angular corners, and most importantly, complete in nature.

As for the specifics of their manifestation, they are progressive in nature and continuously self-complex in settings, with little or no visual input and disturbances. For example, darkness will cause the geometry, but this can immediately be reset to base level by merely turning on a bright light or actively performing a physical task, which requires any level of concentration. Visionary states of Ayahuasca and other forms of DMT produce a full range of high-level states in a style that is more consistent and reproducible than that of any other commonly used entheogen or psychedelic. These effects include transformations, divine imagery—and this particular effect usually contains inner visualizations with scenarios, settings, concepts, and independent-entity contact. They are more common within dark surroundings and can be described as internal in their manifestation, interactive in style, lucid in credibility, and almost exclusively religious, spiritual, mystical, or transcendental in nature.

The auditory effects of Ayahuasca are extraordinarily consistent and exhibit a full range of effects, which commonly includes aural enhancements, auditory visualizations, and audible distortions.

Research has been done that proves the relative physical safety of DMT on (psychologically and physically) stable individuals. Ayahuasca has been studied by various disciplinary groups in Brazil, the USA, and other countries, and it was revealed that in sensible doses in a supervised setting, it presents no negative cognitive, psychiatric, physical, or psychological consequences. In terms of mental health, the exact study revealed that users expressed elevated levels of happiness and health. Ayahuasca is not physically or psychologically addictive, and many users sense a self-regulating quality as to the frequency of use, even though the substance holds no real tolerance and can be used daily if desired.

* * *

Reset to Your Source

The ceremonial ambience is respectful, relaxed, hospitable, supportive, focused, and reverent. The mood is gratifying and positive, not stern or heavy. You will be enriched with a sense of warm fellowship, shared experience, personal inner exploration, healing, transformation, and renewal. At first, you may experience apprehension, anxiety, or fear of the unknown, but this will pass. There is no need for concern. You can feel protected, accepted, loved, and cared for within the sacred circle, except when there is chanting and noble silence is the principle you are asked to maintain. Please enter the ceremonial space quietly. I urge you to help maintain a sacred space by keeping talking and noise to a minimum before the ritual. Participants should wear white or natural clothes (to show the unity of oneness). If you do not have white or off-white clothing, then light pastels are acceptable. Ideally, your clothing should have no writing on it to avoid distractions. The ceremony may last a while, and many changes in temperature are likely to be experienced. This may be a consequence of actual temperature change or your internal process.

The power experienced during the ceremony can be very intense. If you find yourself becoming tense or scared with the unfamiliarity of the experience, relax your muscles, focus on your breathing, and try to open yourself in trust to the experience in the moment. You may find an urge to yawn during the ceremony. This is your body's yearning for increased oxygen and should alert you to the fact that you need to breathe more.

Your experience within the ritual is spiritually guided. You are safe and protected. Let go and allow yourself to surrender and be carried by the divine. You may experience matters you do not understand. Do not try to fit or force them into your existing mental construct. Just let them be and don't judge or justify them. Quiet your thoughts, and maintain an open, natural, and relaxed attitude. Trust that what you are experiencing is occurring to support your healing and transformation.

You are not just a meaningless fragment in an alien universe, briefly suspended between life and death, allowed a few short-lived pleasures followed by pain and ultimate annihilation. Underneath your outer form, you are connected with something so vast, so beautiful, so immeasurable, and so sacred, that it cannot be spoken of—yet I am speaking of

*it now. I am speaking of it now not to give you something to
believe in but to show you how you can know it for yourself.*

— Anonymous

* * *

During the ceremony, you may find that negative thoughts
surface. Negative energy can drag you down you like a rock. Keep
your mind open, aware, and alert, stay in the energy of the current
circle, and remember to breathe. Focus on the vibration of love and
light that is always present deep within.

Ayahuasca is an inner path not only of transcendence but also
of transformation. In other words, I urge you to confront, process,
and transform the challenging energies that might come up during
the process. Transcendence might occur, but not through avoiding the energies and issues that are present in yourself. The work
is a moment of truth, and if the reality is that your personal problems are blocking you from connecting with the divine, it is time
to acknowledge these blockages in humility, allowing the energy to
come through you and surrender your whole being to the divine.

Try to be in your center and keep your spine in proper ana-
tomical alignment; this helps to allow the energy to flow completely
and freely. Additionally, it is always valuable to face the center table
and align yourself with it.

Feel your seat (or feet if you are standing) on the floor, and let
the ground support you. Feel yourself in your body. Breathe all the
way into the ground; relax your neck, shoulders, and belly. Let all
stress and tension subside.

Ask for guidance, clarification, and help when you want it.
Release your troubles to the light or the Earth. Then, open yourself to

intercept what you have meditated for. Trust deeply that your intentions will be taken seriously in the most magical of ways.

The songs that are used in the ceremony provide immense support for transformation, awareness, realization, and an immediate link to the divine. Participating in music allows us to be more present and to breathe more fully and continuously. There are many elements in the songs: rhythm, melody, words, and the energy at their source. They also act as a force of harmony in the works. If we are all focusing on the melody together, in harmony, we surrender our egos and create a unity that is not matched through any other group activity. The words and meanings of the hymns are essential, but more important is the connection that the songs bring about. Often, if we find a given song in our heart without reading the words, the medicine will provide the teaching that song has for us which might only be peripherally related to the actual meanings of the song. After breathing, focusing on and participating in the music is the next most crucial thing you as a participant in the ceremony can do.

The songs often refer to specific representations or aspects of divine consciousness through names. These names originate from a variety of traditions, such as traditional Shamanism, African religions, Hinduism, Buddhism, Christianity, Judaism, Islam, Sufism, and others. Using these representations are a crucial way to navigate the power of divine consciousness, invoking particular aspects or energies, and helping us to remember to be rooted in specific qualities. A person new to this type of experience may have particular associations with these names from past experiences, be they positive or negative that could block their connection to the divine. Initiates are exhorted to let go of their old associations with these names and to be open to the immediate experience as it is in the moment. After all, one primary purpose of the work is to enable each participant to connect with his or her divine guides, regardless of what names of traditions the person may associate them with.

During the process, you may experience dizziness, nausea, or other physical upset, including purging and diarrhea. If you feel the need to purge, use the bucket provided. Allow the purge to happen with gratitude for the healing you are receiving. Try to drop any sense of shame. At the same time, please try to sustain a level of awareness and responsibility during the process of purging so that whatever you purge goes directly into the bucket, garbage can, or toilet, and that you clean yourself properly afterward.

Remember that what you are experiencing, no matter how tough or challenging, is providing you with deep, authentic healing, and you will ultimately be better off. Sometimes people who are new to this experience may get the idea that the challenging feeling they are going through will never go away, that they will feel like that forever. Please, be confident in yourself—absolutely one hundred percent—that whatever feelings come up in the ceremony will pass. When the service ends, you will come back to your normal state.

The most important reminder is that anyone who starts the ritual by partaking of the Ayahuasca agrees to remain until the end. There can be no exceptions to this regulation. It can be disconcerting to everyone involved if anyone leaves the ceremony before its completion. Please stay in the vicinity of the circle until the ritual is complete. During the ritual, if you want to address a practical issue, you should quietly address the facilitator of the ceremony. The second important principle you should commit to is to touch no one during the entire ceremony. The facilitator may use their voice or touch where appropriate for healing, reassurance, guidance, or any matter of coordination, but our concentration at all times should be on our inner work and inner focus. Small talk and conversation may mess with the experience and will lessen its effects both for you and others. This ceremony is deeply personal. Resist the temptation to observe and become involved in what other people are doing. Keep in mind that everything that occurs in an Ayahuasca ceremony in some way influences everyone else present. Talking, too much movement, the slightest sound from electronic devices, and other sounds may be incredibly distracting to others present and significantly interfere with their work. The best way to ensure that everyone has equal space is to tune in to the breath and the music and to stay as quiet and still as possible throughout the ceremony.

It is beneficial to prepare yourself on the physical, mental, and emotional levels to be more open and available to the healing process. This can make a tremendous difference in allowing you to feel as comfortable and harmonious as possible during the ritual. How you get ready and plant an intention for the experience, your seriousness, and commitment to that intention all set the tone for the ceremony itself.

You should get adequate sleep, eat lightly, avoid salty, pickled, and fermented foods like yeast and tofu, abstain from alcohol, sex, intimate physical contact (such as kissing or even masturbating), and natural or man-made medicines for about one to two weeks before the process. It is ideal also to reduce your consumption of media such as television, news, and the internet, as well as good-for-nothing chitchat. You should stick with natural foods as much as possible, avoiding anything artificial. There are some foods that are strongly recommended you avoid for about a week before the ceremony, especially if you are new to the experience. You should avoid foods like cheese and other dairy products, smoked and canned foods, chicken livers, overripe bananas or avocados, dried fruits such as figs, dates, and raisins, citrus fruits in large quantities, beans, chocolate, and soy sauce. It would be best if you eliminated all types of meat, especially red meat and pork, and any other foods that are tough to digest, including bread and pasta, or that are highly processed. It is also ideal to avoid sugar (particularly artificial sweeteners), caffeine, and spices, especially in large quantities. Recommended foods pre- and post-ceremony are almost anything that falls into a light vegetarian diet, including fresh vegetables and fruits, fish or organic poultry if you must, rice, quinoa, whole grains, seeds, nuts (except peanuts), and vegetarian soups (typically useful as a light lunch the day of the ceremony).

In a nutshell, you must avoid any mind/body substances that would cause strong stimulation of senses or cause deep digestive or thinking processes. Instead, the focus must be set on the lightness of existence, your intentions, spiritual practices, and awareness of your perceptions and reactions. Homemade vegan or vegetable soups and stews are an excellent choice.

Yogis usually adopt this philosophy of eating less to stay focused on the lightness of their existence. This also contributes significantly to their intentions of preserving the environment and nature as well. Ghanim Al-Sulaiti, cofounder of Evergreen Organics, has commented on this: "The market supply of food is far greater than the market demand. If you consider that a single supermarket's fridge filled with fresh products will have to be emptied by the end of the day, have you ever asked yourself where will it go? In fact, some produced foods never quite make it on to the market, despite being perfectly fine for us to consume, purely because only the 'best' tends to qualify. We're living in a world where some 795 million people in the world do not have enough food, and yet, while we insist companies change their policies on the single use plastics, or renewable packaging, food waste is often something the population turn a blind eye to... The environmental impact is not necessarily just down to the disposal of excess food, but it's in the resources that have been used to produce those food products, considering energy and natural resources. Recent studies have shown that a plant-based diet cuts the use of land by seventy-six percent and halves the greenhouse gases, reduce landfills and other pollution that are caused by food production. When it comes to water, seventy percent of the world water is being used for agriculture, so when we talk about food waste we talk about loss of fresh water. Our extreme levels of food waste extend so far that it's almost too much to comprehend, given that we are the ones in control of the food demand/supply." We cannot separate our well-being from nature's welfare if our intention is geared toward a united consciousness.

The day of the ceremony, try to nurture the relaxation space by taking it easy and avoiding stressful situations if possible, especially concerning work and finance. Allow yourself to be silent and meditative. Use techniques that can support you with this, such as meditating, yoga, exercising, breathing techniques, dancing, walking, jogging, being in nature, bathing, praying—whatever relaxes you. In any case, having limited food in your digestive system will give the medicine space to work more effectively as well as help to avoid the influence of food-based energies so that you are positively influenced by the medicine. Your last meal should not be less than seven hours before the ceremony. However, don't enter the ceremony hungry. A bowl of light, homemade vegetable soup is ideal.

Also, it would help if you were very well hydrated before the ceremony, so drink two to three liters of water each day for a couple of days beforehand. Make sure you allow yourself enough time for your trip to the ceremony location so that you arrive with time to spare and relaxed. It is also advised to avoid taking most supplements less than seven hours before the ceremony, including vitamins. The day of, it is important that you avoid protein supplements entirely. At all costs, avoid prescription drugs for at least one week prior. All medicated prescription drugs are synthesized with man-made compounds and are very toxic to the natural body.

Drink water and eat some fruit and light food. It is recommended that you empty the water bottle you brought into the ceremony, as the old water will likely contain physical and energy toxins released during the ceremony. Brush your teeth, have a change of clothes, relax, and take it slow. If possible, keep the meditation space for as long as possible so you do not undermine your experience and so you give room for your integration process to occur. Only drive if you feel that the effects of the medicine have entirely worn off and you feel you have enough energy to proceed with your trip. If you feel fatigued, sleep at least two to three hours before getting behind the wheel. You should be able to do that at the ceremony, and remember to take a shower before going to sleep.

Also, be sure to wash your worn clothes before you wear them again. You may choose to save some of your experience to yourself to preserve its sacredness and personal meaning. If you find it helpful to share your experience with others, that is fine, but please do not talk about anyone else's participation but your own. Also, remember that everything that comes from you is reflective of the true atti-tudes you have formed toward yourself and your revered journey, so remember to choose love and full acceptance. Many people discover that the process that starts in the ceremony may continue in earnest for several days afterward, although admittedly on a much subtler level. Remember that you are in a sacred place for that time, and if you can, leave some room in your schedule for solitude to relax and be alone afterward. You can use this time to endorse and integrate what you have received.

Even with an understanding of the science behind DMT and the two plants, it should be understood that the physical knowledge of the medicine does not come close to accurately describing the actual complex interaction of spiritual forces and guidance of the healing process encountered by those who work with the medica-tion in a ritualized setting. It is as if the components of the herb are merely reflecting the spiritual forces, which are embodied within it; this must be experienced to be understood. "You were certainly in unmindfulness of this, and We have removed from you your cover, so your sight, this Day, is sharp." Quran, CH50: V22.

Another crucial thing to realize about this medicine, as opposed to virtually every other well-known state-altering sub-stance, is that Ayahuasca and DMT-have been scientifically proven by many medical institutions including Johns Hopkins-to be one hundred percent non-toxic. The herb has no adverse effect on the body. The opposite is true: it provides deep cleansing on the cellu-lar level of all the bodies, organs, cognitive mind, and systems. The only concerns you should have regarding adverse reactions would be those caused by improper diet, ingestion of synthetic chemicals in certain medicines, or preexisting severe health conditions, especially heart, blood pressure or severe liver problems, asthma, or epilepsy. If you are taking any synthetic prescription medication, please discuss this with the ceremony organizers and a doctor well in advance of the ceremony. The only real journey is your inner journey.

Psychedelics is not a shortcut; it's a path which takes you straight to The Destination of your inner worlds and outer worlds. There is no better truth vehicle. I don't feel there's enough time for psychoanalysis and breaking the doors of perception with the mind alone, that time window has come and gone, unless one is already preconditioned to do so. However, as for the sacred plant medicines they work for those that think they don't work, if the dosage and setting are right, there are truly no limits. There are many philosophers and mystical teachers who have openly admitted to using these sacred plant medicines; these plant medicines contain spirits within them, a teaching spirit, I've never heard of anyone accessing these particular spirits without the plants. One may reach a state of nirvana and hallucination with meditation or practices such as kundalini yoga, but for those who have done the sacred plants, know that what some meditator calls nirvana or satori, is only the starting point for us! The visions that people encounter during these journeys are often deeply symbolic. The origin of all world religions and sacred art traditions is a mystic visionary state. Moses encountered a Burning Bush and heard the voice of God. An angel came to Mary to announce the coming of the holy child growing in her womb. Mohammed rode on the back of Barach, a flying mule, to the seventh heaven. The discovery of the transcendental realm at first astonishes us and then compels us to share that revelation with others. Alex Grey

* * *

Dreaming: The Subconscious State of Mind

What you are is a force—a force that makes it possible
for your body to live, a force that makes it possible
for your whole mind to dream... You are life.

— Don Miguel Ruiz

Is DMT the mainspring of dreams? Since the beginning of time, people were eager to alter their consciousness. They may have desired to gain new or different insights and to see the truth behind things, encounter the divine, and to be conscious of nature. We see traces of psychedelic use across many cultures as well as in shamanic traditions, ancient civilizations, and numerous tales around the world. We have noticed some exciting applications of mind-altering substances throughout history that have revamped our perception of truth in the world around us. What is even more thought-provoking is that humans, plants, animals, and anything with an endorsed consciousness naturally produce these very same substances.

Deep breathing and enchantments have been common cross-cultural practices rehearsed to transcend the mind. Religious and spiritual sacraments involving deep breathing and recitations are correlated with mind-altering ramifications. Although these traditions are often not linked with a psychedelic escapade, a large number of enzymes in our bodies innately transfigure in peculiar ways, and the speculated consequence is DMT induction in the lungs and trace components in the brain. Dr. Rick Strassman has stated on numerous occasions that DMT is generated not only in the lungs but also in other organs of the body. There are over sixty recorded plant breeds encompassing high volumes of DMT that plenty of cultures have consumed to transcend and transform their levels of consciousness. Studies at Johns Hopkins have revealed alternative ways on how to use DMT by the extraction of 5-MeO-DMT from the glands of the bufotenine frog.

Tryptamine, the chemical compound found in DMT, is decidedly significant for sleep. Our brain is an eccentric neural factory that employs and reorganizes chemicals in all sorts of ways. Throughout the day it helps produce serotonin; during nightfall our brains utilize the serotonin to forge melatonin, the hormone responsible for easing our sleep at night. The pineal gland is subliminally connected to our eyes, so as a result of an acute absence of light, the pineal sets in motion a process that transforms serotonin into melatonin. Our brains go through various stages during sleep, when we unconsciously experience different chemical processes that take place. Dreams usually occur during the rapid eye movement (REM) stage of sleep. This often happens when the brain reaches the night's highest levels of melatonin. (Melatonin also regulates the core body temperature, which explains why sleep can be interrupted if it's too cold or too hot.) Once our brains detect these levels of melatonin, it converts the hormone into tryptamine and pinoline. Pinoline is then transmuted into beta-carbolines, and the brain could now integrate the overflowing mix of tryptamine and beta-carbolines, fabricating small quantities of DMT. This indeed may sound like some alchemical sorcery; nevertheless, the medical researcher Dr. Rick Strassman revealed that DMT is indeed connected to the pineal gland and the procedures that take place during REM sleep, has scientifically proved this activity.

It's critical to appreciate the natural, tranquil state of our brain during sleep. The body is primarily immobilized in an unconscious state. Moreover, the minute amounts of DMT produced in the brain are not adequate to induce a full-on DMT experience. Think of it this way: dreaming is like having to drink a cup of tea over a long interval, whereas a full-on DMT experience is like gulping down a hundred shots of black coffee within the same time. There would be a disparity in the physical and mental effects, not because they cause entirely different states, but because one is a considerably magnified version of the other. In spite of the disparities between psychedelic experiences and dreams, some people have encountered psychedelic-like occurrences in their dreams, including out-of-body experiences, kaleidoscopic visualizations, and full-on psychedelic episodes. Often, people who have never used psychedelics before have recounted fractal visuals in dreams which, after using DMT, they confirmed were psychedelic in nature. Most dreams occur during REM, and most REM-based dreams are embodied as mundane human experiences that reflect waking-life events.

On the other hand, as you move down the spectrum of consciousness, DMT experiences are almost always considered as extraordinarily divine, profound, and life-changing encounters with alien dimensions. Lucid dreams, out-of-body and NDE, sleep paralysis, and other REM dreams are all reported to have a more or less similar aftermath as DMT. To conclude my theory, I believe at one end of the scope lies the ego, our materialistic self, and unique identity, and on the other end lies our unified consciousness, a state separated from our body and more integrated with the oneness of the universe. This spectrum is regulated by the induction of DMT in our pineal glands. Low doses of DMT are produced regularly. Certain practices like breath control, meditation, kundalini yoga, and praying generate higher doses of DMT and heighten the probability of transcendence. On very high doses of it, you encounter a life-changing facing down of the truth, that we are not our ego selves. DMT is the spirit vehicle that directs our unique sense of self, or ego, toward believing in a unified consciousness.

CHAPTER 3:
THE EGO

The wound is the place where the Light enters you.

— Rumi

The Ego

Let's have a look at what the ego is and how it's incorporated into the unconscious. *Libido* is a term used in psychoanalysis to explain the energy shaped by survival and sexual instincts. According to Sigmund Freud, the libido is part of the id, the strictly unconscious structure of the psyche comprising love and is the driving force of all behavior. Carl Jung disagreed with Freud regarding the responsibility of sexuality. He was confident that the libido was not utterly for sexual energy but instead traditional psychic energy. For him, the purpose of psychic energy was to stimulate the individual in many vital ways, including spiritually, intellectually, physically, and creatively.

Jung also felt that it was an individual's motivational spring for seeking pleasure and reducing conflict. Interestingly, like Freud, he considered the psyche to be made up of many independent but interacting systems. The three key ones were the ego, the personal unconscious, and the collective unconscious.

Jung clarified that the ego is the conscious mind as it's composed of the memories, thoughts, and emotions a person is mindful of. It is responsible predominantly for feelings of identity and progression. He underlined the importance of the unconscious mind concerning personality and suggested that the unconscious is made up of two layers. The first layer, the personal unconscious, is similar to Freud's interpretation of the unconscious. The personal unconscious encompasses temporally forgotten information as well as suppressed memories. Jung outlined an essential aspect of the personal unconscious called complexes. A complex is a reservoir of thoughts, memories, attitudes, and feelings that aim at a single concept. The more facets attached to the complex, the higher its impact on the individual. Freud suggested that the personal unconscious is shaped with what we add to the complex during our childhood only, while Jung was less concerned with repressed childhood experiences. It is the past *and* present, which in his perspective was the key to both the inspection of neurosis and its treatment.

The purpose of life, as far as I can tell, is to find a mode of being that's so meaningful that the fact that life is suffering is no longer relevant.

— Jordan B. Peterson

* * *

However, by far the most significant distinction between Jung and Freud is Jung's theory of the collective unconscious. This is Jung's most original and debatable offering to personality theory. It is a degree of the unconscious shared with the rest of the human species including dormant, untapped memories from our familial history. "The form of the world into which [a person] is born is already inborn in him, as a virtual image." Carl Jung. As stated by Jung, the mind has inherent characteristics imprinted on it as a product of evolution. These general tendencies stem from our inherited past. Fear of the dark or insects or snakes might be case in point, and it is intriguing that this idea has lately been resurrected in the theory of prepared conditioning. In spite of that, more important than different tendencies are those facets of the collective unconscious that have matured into distinct subsystems of the personality. Jung called these images archetypes and memories. Archetypes are thoughts and images which have the same worldwide meanings across civilizations and cultures and which may be conveyed in dreams, art, literature, or religion. He considered signs and symbols from varying cultures often almost identical because they surfaced from archetypes shared by the human race as a whole, and that is part of our collective unconscious.

According to Jung, our primitive past turns into the cornerstone of the human psyche, regulating and orchestrating present behavior. Jung identified numerous archetypes but granted special attention to four in particular. The persona (or mask) is the external face we demonstrate to the outside world. It obscures our real self, and he explains it as the "conformity" archetype. It is the public face or character a person displays to others.

The second archetype, "anima/animus," is the mirror image of our biological gender; that is, the unconscious feminine half in males and the masculine half in females. Both genders manifest attitudes and behavior of the other by generations of living together. The psyche of a woman contains masculine traits (the animus archetype), and the psyche of a man contains feminine traits (the anima archetype).

The third type is the "shadow." This is the animalistic part of our personality. It is the root of both our destructive and our creative energies. In support of evolutionary theory, it could be that his archetypes reveal predispositions of survival value in the past.

The final one is the "self" that provides a sense of unity in a habitual experience. For Jung, the underlying intent of every individual is to attain a state of selfhood (similar to Maslow's self-actualization), and in this regard, Jung inspired the notion of a humanist nature.

That was undoubtedly Jung's ideology, and in his book *The Undiscovered Self*, he suggests that hordes of modern-life problems are a result of "man's progressive alienation from his instinctual foundation." Additionally, he claimed that the archetypes are products of the collective experience of both genders living together. Despite that, in modern Western civilization, men have been dissuaded from exposing their feminine side and women from expressing their masculine tendencies. The repercussion is that the expansive psychological development of both sexes has been sabotaged. Together with the current patriarchal culture of Western society, this has contributed to the devaluation of feminine qualities overall, and the prevalence of the persona (the mask) has created an insincerity in most people's everyday lives.

Jung's concepts have not been as favored as Freud's, perhaps because he did not write as a layperson and his views were not as widely publicized as Freud's. Furthermore, it might have been because his ideas were more mystical and esoteric. Despite that, more people are beginning to relate to Jung's theories now.

Modern psychology has not been gentle in its scrutiny of Jung's theory of archetypes. Freud's biographer Ernest Jones said that Jung "descended into a pseudo-philosophy out of which he never emerged," and his notions struck philosophers as new-age mystical theories rather than scientific advancements in psychology. Perhaps his mystical doctrines are paying off now that we are piercing the new age.

While Jung's research into ancient mythology, his enthusiasm for astrology, and his obsession with Eastern religions cannot be ignored, it is worth mentioning that, as a matter of historical evidence, the archetypical images he was referring to have captured the human imagination. Also, Jung himself argues that the frequent recurrence of symbols from mythology in therapy back up his hypothesis of an innate, collective cultural remnant.

On the flip side, his work has contributed to general psychology as well. He was the first to discern the two important orientations of personality, extroversion and introversion. Moreover, he distinguished four basic cognitive functions (thinking, feeling, sensing, and intuiting) which, in a cross-classification with the first dichotomy (extraversion and introversion), delivered sixteen independent personality types. Plenty of psychologists like Hans Eysenck and Raymond Cattell have since built upon this. Myers and Briggs built on his theories to bring about the MBTI (their personality type indicator), a tool used today for many purposes. Apart from being a cultural icon for generations of psychology undergraduates, Jung introduced concepts which have been essential to the development of modern personality theory.

*　*　*

Defensive Ego

The ego customarily protects itself from distressing feelings. We don't feel safe within ourselves, although that may seldom be obvious. We often are defending ourselves, in one way or another, from some hurt. Psychologists call this self-protection *defense*. (If you imagine your identity as an entity separate from your soul, you'll be able to understand the concept much better.) Our identity perceives threatening circumstances or feelings as attacks that we need to defend ourselves from. It is the ego's primary activity. During conflicts or disputes, the response is to protect ourselves from feeling hurt, particularly when they escalate into fights and quarrels. It appears more noticeable in others than in ourselves that this self-protection can be more significant than the truth. The other person often appears to be making statements that we are totally convinced aren't true. It appears that they say these things to defend themselves, and they should know they aren't in fact accurate either. Nevertheless, everyone feels the ever-present urge to protect their identity from emotional pain by inflicting it onto the other during arguments. The perceived truth is the first thing that goes out the window to make room for the prevailing ego. In Hebrew, the ego is referred to as *Yetzar Hara* or *destructive force*. It is the self-centered, instant gratification part of your personality that covers your pure essence, like mud on a windshield. It appears when you are born and dies along with the body. It has no compassion for anyone else and is always there when you are mad, stressed, or sad. When you look back at all the stupid decisions you have made, you can be sure that your ego was doing the talking. It is mentioned in the Torah "The ego is like a giant man holding a battle axe who is standing in front of you at a crossroad. The fool is frightened and runs for his life. The wise person looks closely and sees that the giant has no feet. He walks right past him." That's the ego in simple terms—all bark and no bite. The secret of disarming the ego is by having clarity that it is only an illusion. If ego is the mud covering the windshield of the soul, then clarity is the water that rinses it away.

Blaming is usually a part of conflicts. When a person blames us for something, we may be inclined to blame that person back. Sometimes, the other person is accusing us of prejudice. Although sometimes what's happening is that we can't endure the guilt, we blame them just because we feel one of the parties has to be condemned and there's no room for common grounds. Accusing the person that they're only defending themselves, and as a result not seeing the truth, will generally have the effect of that person defending themselves even more rigorously. The need to defend is hugely compelling.

However, even when we are not in an obvious conflict, we will still continually defend ourselves. Our egos have quite a few ways of doing that. Once we detect that we are about to feel hurt, we may get tense, our blood starts to boil, and we can feel it rush into our head, preventing us from reason. When we are not relaxed, we are usually evading some terrible feeling or perhaps nauseating sensations. We embrace one feeling to steer clear from the other. When we get infuriated but don't want to act livid toward the other person, it may be excruciatingly tough to shut down the anger. Angry reactions will keep occurring. We got angry because we were harmed. The rationale behind not putting an end to anger is that we'd have to recognize the unexpressed repulsive sensations that provoked the outrage in the first place, and we don't want to go through that. So, we react impulsively. We can also deny feeling anything altogether. When we desire to be with a person but it is not mutual, we may determine that we don't admire that person after all. That's not entirely true, but it does make life more tolerable.

This defensive mechanism makes us very anxious with what is outside of us, with how we seem to be to other people. It makes it more difficult to recognize what goes on inside us, within our inner soul. When we are contemplating and reflecting, we don't feel much of what happens with our subtler feelings, we only recognize and get in touch with the feelings that surface, if at all. Isolating and withdrawing deep into ourselves, therefore, is a way of keeping unpleasant feelings at bay. Our constant, obsessive concern with self-protection leads to feeling numb by the time we become adults. Every so often, it can appear dangerous to feel anything at all. We then end up with a constantly flat state of mind. Some people will refute that those feelings are a real part of who they are and consider themselves one hundred percent–rational individuals, which only leads to them losing touch with their inner self even more.

The consequence of all these defensive strategies is that we're not really in touch with our essence. We can't know ourselves when we don't allow ourselves to feel. Consequently, we are unaware of why we are behaving the way we do. The instant a self-protective reaction makes it impossible to deal with our deeper feelings, these feelings stay hidden, repressed, and unresolved. They disappear into our unconscious but do not cease to affect us. Eventually, the defensive ego will grow with us as we age; hence, surrendering to our essence becomes more challenging, and the tendency to not believe in unity increases. It's no surprise that kids have so much faith in God in their early stages of development: their egos haven't yet developed, nor have their repressed feelings aggregated to a degree where they resist the idea of a divine source from which we all stem as one. Social conditioning and cultural programming unfetter children, even though their unconscious is highly susceptible at these early stages; they are still closer to the source of unconditional love than the culturally programmed predispositions allow for. It all begins when we start confining and programming their behavior. Dr. Mohamud A. Verjee is the assistant dean of Medical Student Affairs, an associate professor of family medicine in clinical medicine, the consultant family physician at Weill Cornell Medicine-Qatar, and an adjunct associate professor of family medicine in the Department of Family Medicine at the University of Calgary in Canada. He says, "The fact that we are born dependent on others from birth is obvious. How we shape as children, grow into adolescence, and adulthood is unwritten. When we question our existence, we get to the soul of our being. Many have asked about their purpose in life as if there was any predestined goal or objective. What matters, in reality, is our freedom to develop and design a pathway of discovery in life, whether it be humble or grander. Investing in the thought that we are all potentially equal is not the same as saying that we all have an equal chance. Opportunities for education and unforeseeable experiences will tailor our thoughts as well as the people who surround us. We have a brief time period on this Earth to learn, teach, deliver, live, love, and procreate. There is no formula or blueprint to follow. That is the inspiration, to forge an individual life of utility in the hope that posterity will ultimately benefit. In the process, we should not forget to have faith, both in God and ourselves, whatever the outcome of our abilities."

Unconscious Mind: What It Is and How It Works

Although most people believe that what goes on inside them is pretty straightforward, everyone has a blind spot: the unconscious. This is a part of us which we aren't aware of but which influences almost all of our actions and feelings. Of all the things we do or feel, we do not know where they come from, even if they feel part of our nature. We can sometimes notice pieces of the unconscious or what it makes us do or feel. We may start feeling sad, happy, scared, energetic, or angry for no apparent reason, despite the fact it does appear to make sense deep inside. As adults, sometimes we may start feeling like a child (and perhaps try to combat that feeling, right?). We may even feel numbness and a void, in a flat state all the time, when we reminisce that this was not the case when we were kids. We may be preoccupied with specific thoughts for long periods. We may daydream about pleasant memories from the past or things that might supervene in the future. We can stay resentful about things far longer than reasonable. Even when we realize that this doesn't help us in any way, we are not able to stop doing it. It's as if we are jammed. We quite frequently feel the necessity to protect or defend ourselves from some emotional burn. While this urge feels quite real, we often cannot identify what it is precisely in us that needs protection. We have traditional ways of reacting to certain situations that most of us take for granted. It appears that we are that way, even when we suppose some of these patterns are not very helpful in living our lives contentedly.

Some people manage to get under our skin and make us do things we had no intention of doing. When that doesn't happen by an explicit display of force, we may even have no idea what made us react this way; we are sensitive to manipulation. There are various things we believe we should or should not feel or do. We are only conscious of what we should, and we feel pressured to comply. Besides, we tend to abide by a vague sense of rules without giving it much thought; it just seems to happen instinctively. All of these things source from the unconscious. When we don't realize why we are feeling a certain way, this is when we are not in sync and not aware of a part of ourselves, the unconscious.

We suppress feelings, trying not to deal with them if they are dreadful, negative, or uncomfortable—even overwhelming. We might think it's weak to feel fear, so we end up suppressing our apprehension instead of associating with it. Then again, we may convince ourselves that it's wrong to be enraged or to experience hatred; hence, we end up smothering such emotions. It may be intolerable to cope with rejection or withstand hurt, so we do what it takes to preserve ourselves. However, when we do that, we are burying feelings into the unconscious. Feelings don't go away when we repress them; they are bottled up in our unconscious. Even though we are no longer conscious of them, they still influence and control us. Our behavior and responses are affected by the quashed feelings, and we will keep having thoughts that are linked to them.

Much of our unconscious was shaped and molded during infancy. As a young child, we were exposed to many overwhelming experiences, and instead of dealing with the feelings associated with these experiences, we were taught to put a lid on them through discipline and manipulation. In the course of our upbringing, we were obliged to learn how to deal with people, behave around family, manage friends, and cope with society. Becoming proficient in the process was a painful undertaking that led to a fair number of suppressed feelings. All this sowed the seeds of our unconscious that we have to live with for the remainder of our lives.

We don't only conceal feelings in our unconscious but also our compounded outlook and overall viewpoints of accumulated situations and the mechanism of behaving in them. In the present, we access these memories of past experiences and render the patterns of behavior accordingly. We arrogate distinct roles from these patterns in response to constant exposure and repetition. We react spontaneously and thoughtlessly, precisely as we used to in the past.

These patterns are elicited by how we feel at the moment. For instance, when we stumble on a situation that has let us down, a pattern may emerge based on a previous experience that made us feel disappointed. We then deal with the current situation as we did with the previous one. If we got intensely bitter during the last disappointment, we might become bitter again subconsciously, whether the circumstances require it or not, and it doesn't have to make sense.

Someone who went through a stressful or traumatic encounter in a crowded and confined area during their childhood may now become petrified in full elevators or even develop claustrophobia relative to the severity of their early trauma. These compilations make us utterly predictable and unaware of why we cling to behavioral patterns like that. It may make us gullible to manipulation by others. It is the essence of our egos. The reason we don't detect the process of suppressing memories that influence our current behavior is that part of the mind is the suppressor itself. We then replicate the pattern of suppression. Hence, we continue forgetting and find ourselves in a vicious cycle that becomes impenetrable.

Freud was praised for bringing light to the unconscious. On the other hand, in the Eastern world, the existence of the unconscious has been known a while longer. Various meditation techniques and spiritual connections with one's core have long been used to return to a state of self-awareness, free of ego.

> *The spiritual journey often looks like a dance between*
> *the two distinct poles of vulnerability and boundaries.*
> *It's a continuing dialogue between the impulse to soften*
> *and open and the impulse to contain and protect. The*
> *two apparent opposites turn out to be equal partners*
> *in the process of embodying spirit and heart.*

— Sally Kempton

*   *   *

The Superego

The superego makes us adhere to social norms. The superego consumes a solid section of our unconscious. It is the portion of us that makes us comply with rules and laws, that coerces us to behave. The superego is also responsible for judging, criticizing, and shaming us when we violate a code of conduct. It's what makes us feel guilty, embarrassed, humiliated, and apologetic. It is our inner judge and inner critic.

Our superego instructs us how not to be impudent to people, but rather respectful. It guides us to heed etiquette and to be industrious, cooperative, and obedient, and if we don't conform, it judges us. Moreover, it's responsible for feelings related to indignity, dishonor, stupidity, and foolishness; that is, of course, if we do not repress these bad feelings. While the superego has our best interests at heart, it is not very amicable in nature. We rarely notice the superego controlling how we act. We sense that we shouldn't be doing questionable acts, and we shy away from them. Most of it is, in reality, unconscious.

The superego is shaped during our childhood. Our parents taught us what moral values were, what we should and shouldn't do, what was reasonable and what was not. To get us to follow the rules, we were subdued and molded through either subtle or devious means, such as punishments, disgrace, shame, or humiliation, for doing something wrong, inappropriate, dishonest, dishonorable, or unethical. Such endeavors shape the superego. It's not only our parents but many other people in our early surroundings that intimidated us into conforming to specific rules— teachers, adults in other positions of authority, as well as children our age. The superego is the accumulation of effects from everyone who restrained us into conforming to a set of rules and regulations in the past. People still coerce us when we are adults: they act out their superegos on us, as we do on them. Children aren't capable of realizing the consequences of their actions. They need to be guided and educated as to how to abide by rules, or else they would get hurt or—worse still—hurt others, damage things, or do something else wrong. They need to be trained to take responsibility for their actions. Therefore, it is inevitable and undoubtedly beneficial that children instigate a superego. It has to guide people's lives.

When you feel like you're drowning in life, don't
worry, your lifeguard walks on water.

— Anonymous

We need to be aware that sometimes when we feel guilty about something, it's a false alarm and, in reality, there is nothing wrong at all. We may feel stupid for not knowing to do something when in fact we never actually had a chance to learn it. Children are notorious for feeling unreasonably guilty for the death of family members or parents divorcing. Sometimes a situation requires us to be assertive. The superego isn't entirely precise; it may prevent us from doing certain things when sometimes there is nothing wrong with them. Thus, it is an aspect that can limit us more than required at times.

Although we ultimately want to be ourselves, we often are not. We reject our feelings when they are distressing, fallacious, or defensive. We need to be ourselves to be truly happy. Being happy is an internal matter and is not related to or limited to external factors. It may seem inexplicable or clichéd, but to be satisfied we need to let in and embrace our unpleasant feelings. How can we be happy when we're not genuine or wholly self, discontented with the emotions that are deep inside? If we don't authorize access in its entirety to our feelings, we can only experience a warped sense of happiness, with agonizing suffering going on under the surface, leaking into our consciousness every so often. Undesired feelings remain forever if we suppress them. They will continue to exist in our unconscious. If we do allow ourselves to feel the unwanted as they arise at any given moment, they'll run their natural way, meaning that they'll dissolve in due course. This doesn't necessarily condone acting on them, though that can help in particular instances to trigger awareness.

* * *

The Paralyzed Soul: Falling in Love with Your Fragile Ego (Narcissistic Self)

When it comes to identifying whether a person is a narcissist, most people make it more difficult than need be. I use the cat test—that is, if it looks like a cat and meows like a cat, it probably is a cat. There are no blood tests, X-rays, or exact measurements that can diagnose narcissism. Even therapists have to justify their observations of the attitudes, behaviors, and reactions that an individual displays to label it narcissism. What makes it easier is the fact that we understand precisely what a narcissist resembles. According to the *Diagnostic and Statistical Manual of Mental Disorders*, which therapists use as a guide, a person needs to display only fifty-five percent of the properties described below to be deemed narcissistic.

The world of the narcissist revolves around good or bad, superior or inferior, and right or wrong. There's a massive surge of superiority and entitlement instilled within the person. There is a well-defined hierarchy, with the narcissist at the summit—it is the only place they feel safe. Narcissists have to be the most right, the best, and the most qualified. They own everything, do everything their way, and control everyone. Paradoxically, narcissists can acquire that superior feeling by being the worst: the most ill, most upset or most injured for a period. Then they believe they're entitled to receive comforting attention and even the right to hurt you or to command apologies to make things even. They are usually experts in blaming and deflecting accusations. Although narcissists want to be in full control, they never want to be responsible for the consequences unless everything goes exactly their way and their desired result takes place.

When someone doesn't conform to their plan, or they feel scrutinized or less than perfect, the narcissist lays the entire blame and responsibility on others. It has to be someone else's fault, never theirs. At other times, the narcissist selects a specific person to blame—their mother, their in-laws, or anyone who restricts their goals. They most likely blame the one person who is the most emotionally attached, loyal, and loving person in their life, and the safest person to blame is the one who is least likely to leave or reject them. You've probably fallen into the trap of attempting to reason and use logic with such a person to get them to understand the painful effect their behavior has on you. You believe that if they could discern how much their behavior hurt you, they'd change. Your pleading, unfortunately, falls on deaf ears, as narcissists are only capable of being aware of their thoughts and feelings. Even though they may assume they understand, they genuinely don't. Therefore, they execute their decisions based on how they feel about something, not how others feel. They invariably go to someone else to resolve their feelings and needs. They expect you to abide by their ways, and they behave with irritation and resentment if you don't.

Since they are frequently dissatisfied with the imperfect channels life unveils, they crave doing as much as possible to control it and bend it to their desire. They insist on being in control, and their sense of superiority makes it logical that they be the one in control of everything. Narcissists always have a script in mind about what each person in their field of communication should be doing and saying. When you don't function as anticipated, they become considerably upset and critical. They can't grasp the way forward, as you've gone off script. They demand that you do precisely what they want so they can arrive at their desired outcome. You are a pawn in their chess game, not a real person with your own thoughts and feelings. They can't see where they end and you begin. They are very similar to children and believe that they're entitled to everything and that everyone should think and feel the same way they do and have the same aspirations as they do. They are offended and insulted when people object. If a narcissist wants something from you, great lengths will be undertaken to get it, through persistence, coaxing, demanding, frowning, manipulating, or rejecting.

Moreover, narcissists have a notably high expectation of perfection. They consider they must be perfect, as must you, events should proceed as accurately as expected, and life should roll out exactly as they envisioned. This is an excruciatingly impossible command; consequently, they end up feeling disappointed and troubled almost all the time. The desire for perfection leads them to protest, criticize, and be continuously miserable. Stress is a constant, nebulous feeling that something terrible is occurring or about to take place. Some narcissists expose their anxiety by always talking about the destruction that is about to happen, while some hide and suppress their stress. Most narcissists project their fear onto their loved ones, accusing them of being unsupportive, mentally ill, negative, not responding to their needs or putting them first, or being self-absorbed and selfish. All this is intended to extend their anxiety onto those closest to them in an endeavor to manipulate the other and ultimately not feel stressed themselves. The narcissist feels better and gains strength and superiority, while you feel your anxiety and depression build.

Narcissists have an exaggerated need for attention and validation, always saying something to grab your attention. Validation for them doesn't count as enough when it's coming from others; their desire for validation is like a funnel, as you spill in positive, supportive, and comforting statements, and they flow out the other end and are flushed down the toilet, leaving you with nothing! No matter how much you tell them you love them or admire them, it's never enough because deep down they don't think anyone can love them. Despite all their self-centered, grandiose, egotistical bragging, narcissists are very insecure and afraid of not measuring up. They try unceasingly to extract praise and endorsement from others to buoy their delicate egos, but no matter how much they're granted, they always demand more. Narcissists have limited ability to empathize with others. They tend to be remarkably selfish, self-absorbed, and habitually unable to intuit what others are feeling. They expect others to behave and feel the same way they do and hardly give any thought to how others feel. They are also seldom apologetic or repentant.

Although narcissists are very sensitive to insinuated threats, anger, and rejection, as a result they frequently misinterpret subtle emotions and are typically biased toward translating facial expressions as negative. Unless you are throwing a tantrum, they won't precisely discern what you're feeling. They are completely blind and oblivious to other people's inner emotions. Despite someone saying *I'm sorry* or *I love you* when the narcissist is on edge or bitter, they can fire back surprisingly harshly. Furthermore, if your words and facial expressions aren't aligned in message, they will likely mistake the communication. This is why narcissists frequently confuse sarcasm for an intentional factual statement. Their lack of capacity to accurately read body language and interpret feelings are some reasons why they are mostly apathetic about others.

Narcissists also lack an understanding of the essence of feelings. They don't recognize how their feelings transpire. They think someone or some external stimuli influence their emotions. They don't comprehend that their feelings are produced by their biochemistry, unconscious thoughts, and conscious interpretations. Furthermore, they perpetually believe their emotions are a result of your behaviors—particularly the negative ones. They assume that because you didn't follow their plan or because you made them feel vulnerable, you are the one to blame. The absence of empathy makes authentic relationships and emotional connection with them painful and almost impossible to bear. Narcissists don't feel guilty because they imagine they are always right, and they don't think their behaviors influence others. However, they do hold onto a sense of shame, which is the notion that there is something enduringly wrong or unethical about who they are as a role model. Buried in a deeply suppressed unconscious of the narcissist are all the insecurities, fears, and rejected traits that they are always on guard to conceal from everyone, including themselves. The narcissist is severely ashamed of all these rejected thoughts and emotions.

They tend to divide everything in their relationships and compartmentalize it all into good and bad elements. Any negative behaviors are blamed on you or others; on the other hand, they seek credit for everything that is positive and good. They deny their cruel words and acts, while continuously accusing you of opposing them for no reason. They also identify things as entirely good and pure or as evil and repulsive. They can't seem to blend these two constructs. The narcissist's whole life is fortified by fear—mostly buried and suppressed. They're always afraid of being scorned or rejected. They may have concerns about losing all their money, being emotionally or physically attacked, being abandoned, or being seen as unfit or incompetent. This makes it challenging and sometimes impossible for them to trust anyone.

The more closely your relationship evolves, the less they will trust you. Narcissists fear any genuine intimacy or vulnerability as they're afraid you'll discern their imperfections and reject them. No matter how much you reassure them, it seems to not make a difference. Narcissists genuinely despise and deny their aggressive shortcomings. They never seem to trust in the love of others, and they continuously test you with ever-worse behaviors in an attempt to find your breaking point. Their compulsive fear of being found out or abandoned never disappears. Keeping their vulnerabilities protected is essential to their pretentious, false self. However, this makes it impossible for them to be entirely authentic and transparent.

* * *

Your task is not to seek for love, but merely to seek and find
all the barriers within yourself that you have built against it.

— Rumi

Because of their failure to deal with feelings, their persistent urge for self-protection, and their lack of empathy, narcissists can't love purely or connect emotionally with anyone. They cannot perceive the world from others' perspectives. They're emotionally isolated and oblivious. When one relationship is not gratifying anymore, they often hang on to relationships long after their dissolution or they start a new one as soon as they can. Uncaring about others, they want people to feel their pain, to sympathize with them, and make everything just as they want it to be. They have minimal capacity to respond to others' anxiety, fear, or need for care and sympathy.

Thoughtful, accommodating behaviors need a firm understanding of each other's feelings. Will this move make both of us happy? How will the other person feel? How will this change our relationship? Don't expect the narcissist to understand these questions, give in to them, or give up anything they want for your benefit: it's pointless.

Happiness is the only thing that multiplies when it's shared.

— Albert Schweitzer

* * *

Narcissistic Parents

A narcissistic parent can be characterized as a person who lives through, is possessive of, and is involved in trivialized competition with their child. Usually, such a parent regards the independence of a child (and adult children) as a threat and orders the child to subsist in their shadow, with unreasonable expectations. In a narcissistic parenting relationship, the child is seldom loved for being themselves but for what the adult wants them to be.

Various studies have been carried out about narcissistic parenting and the repercussions for children. Separating certain parent centric tendencies from chronic narcissistic parenting is essential. Many parents want to showcase their children, have high expectations, may be firm at times (such as when a child is misbe-having), and urge their child to make them proud. None of these qualities alone comprise malevolent narcissism. What distinguishes the narcissistic parent is a prevalent tendency to deny the child, even as an adult, a sense of independent selfhood. The child lives solely to serve the needs and plots of the parent. Unfortunately, the adult is entirely oblivious to how these behaviors impact the child, espe-cially during adolescence. Consequently, a narcissistic parent may put the child down so that they might maintain their superiority. Examples of this type of competitive marginalization include biased judgment and criticisms, improper comparisons, lack of validation for positive behaviors and sentiments, and rejection of accomplish-ments and success.

Some common put-downs include statements like: *There's always something wrong with you, You'll never be good enough*, and *If you are not a doctor or engineer, then your career is insignificant.* While lowering the child's confidence, the narcissistic parent con-sequently gets to raise their insecure self-worth. Many narcissistic parents have an erroneously inflated self-image, with an arrogance about who they are and what they do. People around the narcissist are usually not treated as human beings but as a means to an end. Frequently, their children are objectified, while others are molded to hold the same, forged superiority obsession: *We're better than they are.* This sense of grandiosity, though, is virtually based on superfi-cial, egotistical, and materialistic trappings, obtained at the expense of one's humanity, relatedness, and conscientiousness. One can only become more superior by being less human. Always remember, *thou shalt love thy neighbour as thyself.* Bible, CH22: V40.

Similarly related to grandiosity, many narcissistic parents love to announce to others how special they are. They enjoy publicly exhibiting what they consider their superior qualities, be they material possessions, projects, physical appearance, accomplishments, familial background, contacts in high positions, or a trophy spouse and children. They go out of their way to solicit ego-boosting attention and flattery.

All parents want their children to succeed. However, some narcissistic parents set expectations not in the child's best interest but for the realization of their selfish dreams and needs. Instead of raising a child with thoughts, emotions, and goals that are appreciated and valued, the youth becomes an extension of their parent's hopes, and their originality is diminished. Since such a parent frequently hopes that the child will permanently reside under their influence, they may become very jealous at any hints of maturation and independence. Any distinct act of individuation and separation, from choosing one's academic and career track to making nonapproved friends to spending time on their priorities are evaluated negatively and personally. In the eyes of a narcissistic parent, no romantic partner is ever good enough for their child, and no intruder can ever challenge them for dominance; otherwise, they'll be responded to with rejection, criticism, and competition. A well-known theme operating through these modes of manipulation is that love is only given as a conditional reward and not the natural affection of healthy parenting. As a result, the withholding of love is used as a threat or punishment: *I am doing everything for you, and you're ungrateful.*

Some narcissistic parents are very rigid when it comes to the desired behaviors of their children. They control their youth in the minutest detail and can be shocked and disconcerted when there's a slight deviation. Narcissistic parents are also irritable and quickly triggered. Reasons for sensitivity toward a child can vary considerably, from the child's lack of attention, compliance, and submission to faults and deficiencies or being in the presence of the parent at the wrong time. One reason for the parent's inflexibility and sensitivity might be the desire to control their offspring. Narcissists respond negatively and disproportionally when they see that the strings will not always pull the child. These parents expect their child to take care of them for the rest of their lives and communicate that obligation to them. This kind of dependency can be physical, emotional, and financial. While there's nothing innately wrong with taking care of older parents—it's an admirable undertaking and often an unquestionable duty—the narcissistic parent usually manipulates the child into making unreasonable sacrifices and compromises, with limited regard for their priorities, needs, and wants.

In extreme situations, a narcissistic parent may prioritize their selfish interests, which to the narcissist are even more compelling than raising the child. These activities may give the adult the stimulation, self-importance, and validation they crave, be it career obsession, social position, or personal interests. The child is either left alone or with the other parent. One of the most obvious indications of a narcissistic father or mother is the failure to be mindful of the child's thoughts and feelings and validate them as real and vital. Only what the parent thinks and feels is important; children under this sort of authority may react over time with one of three survival instincts. One is to fight back and stand up for themselves. Flight is an option, where they distance themselves from their parent(s). Some, however, may freeze and replace their invalidated real self with a hollow persona, hence adopting characteristics of narcissism themselves.

You must purge yourself before finding faults in others.
When you see a mistake in somebody else, try to find
if you are making the same mistake. This is the way
to take judgment and turn it into improvement.

— B. K. S. Iyengar

* * *

Narcissistic In-Laws

We are shaped by the people who matter to us. It is imperative to recognize what is happening inside us and how the outside world views
us. If we don't get out of our bubble and perceive ourselves with
external eyes, we won't be able to get along with the most important
characters that may eventually come into our lives, our in-laws. Our
in-laws can be a source of bliss or misery in our life. Not everybody
gets along with their spouse's parents. Indeed, this is the base of a
traditional piece of humor around the world, but it is a lot less enter-
taining if their behavior stops being merely annoying and becomes
toxic. Let's look into why things go downhill with in-laws. It's critical
that we identify the source of the predicament to be able to make
peace with ourselves and others. There are common disputes that
might point to where they stand. Contrarily, dealing with in-laws
takes diplomacy and a united front between us and our companion.
We have to learn how to establish boundaries and independence to
preserve ourselves and understand how to face and deal with any
problems. Confrontation with parents-in-law may not seem appealing most of the time, so we choose to avoid conflicts, only to find
them multiply. Dr. Mohamud A. Verjee counsels thus: "If you want

to realize a dream, never stop dreaming or give up your goals. When faced by failure, find an ethical way to convert the negative into a positive, then savor that achievement with humility." Don't be hesitant to talk with your companion about setting healthy boundaries with both families. It's uncomfortable but required. Isn't love splendid?

Follow your bliss and the universe will open
doors where there were only walls.

— Joseph Campbell

* * *

The issue of the narcissistic in-law needs some explanation: it's not only just that they demand to be the center of attention at all times. As psychotherapist Michelle Piper describes, being in a relationship with the child of a narcissist suggests threatening one of the parent's extensions of "narcissistic supply"; they affirm their status and self-worth through their child. Narcissist in-laws will argue furiously against this extension being taken away from them and despise the fact that the young partner is shifting the spotlight. The spouse will never be good enough, and they will spend a considerable time informing them of that.

After years of feeding a parent's ego, children often reach adulthood without a clear sense of self. For narcissists, it is often displayed through the status of their children and their supposed success as a parent. Narcissism ranges from a personality characteristic, like extraversion or self-confidence, to full-fledged malevolent narcissist. A malevolent narcissist is usually self-centered and preoccupied with an urge to attain the perfect image (recognition, status, power) and has no capacity for listening, caring, or even recognizing the needs of others.

Dr. Keith Campbell confirms, in his book the *Narcissism Epidemic*, that narcissists have high levels of self-absorption, distrust, perfection, entitlement, grandiosity, and emotional detachment that impair their functioning and last an extensive period. According to Karyl McBride in her book *Will I Ever be Free of You*, during tough times the daughter (for instance) of a narcissistic parent may end up codependent and stifling her partner with overwhelming demands, jealousy, and insecurities, and will need him to meet all her requirements, especially her emotional ones. When he can't, she will hold the same disappointment and emptiness she did as a child and blame him. The good news is that it can get better; the bad news is that they are not the only one who was raised by a narcissistic parent and went into love and commitment ill-equipped. According to Campbell, almost ten percent of young adults in their twenties display enough traits to be classified as narcissists.

Narcissists' focus may be on achievement or status, but either way, when it comes to their child, the attention is more on what they do with their life as opposed to who they are. In the parent's eyes, everything the younger person does returns to them. Instead of being loved and nurtured, the child has the burden of carrying the spotlight around and shining it on their parent.

Wendy Behary, founder and director of the Cognitive Therapy Center of New Jersey and Schema Therapy Institute, explains in her book *Disarming the Narcissist*, that children who have grown up with narcissistic parents walk around believing that the only value they possess is to meet everybody else's expectations. McBride describes the child of a narcissistic parent's relationship as a legacy of distorted love, based on "what I can do for you or what you can do for me".

McBride further explains that when the daughter of a narcissist starts a relationship, she may search for someone that she can take care of but unfortunately end up in a codependent relationship. These ladies may choose men who are narcissists as well, or who can't love them for who they are. Wendy Behary confirms that the way daughters of narcissists select partners is very similar to people who grow up with abuse. The child might reenact the pattern that they knew as a child. Hence, they move from a narcissistic parent to a narcissistic partner. Sam Vaknin, the author of *Malignant Self Love, Narcissism Revisited*, calls this "counter-dependency." Counter-dependents fear intimacy and are locked into hesitant cycles of approach followed by avoidance of commitment.

Furthermore, if the child does choose a partner, their parent focuses on their superficial attributes, such as looks, money, education, job title, or possessions instead of compatibility and emotional health. This can hinder the relationship's progress. Initial visits to meet the parents will feel more like job interviews than friendly family gatherings. This is not uncommon. Behary explains that partners feel as if they're always under the microscope, being evaluated and judged for the slightest mistakes. Fearing eternal judgment and the parent's intrusion into every aspect of their lives, the companion's feelings for his partner might not be enough. In the end, they'll decide that there's no way they can be together. After numerous failed attempts, they might stay together and try to work things out. They'll fluctuate between dependency and codependency, entitlement and blame. This occurs due to fear of abandonment and as affirmation of the parent that the child is making unfit choices.

When you realize nothing is lacking, the
whole world belongs to you.

— Lao Tzu

* * *

According to Vaknin, children of narcissists fear relationship failure and abandonment: they couldn't bear the thought of telling their parent that they failed, and they might feel coerced to accept relationship red flags or bail from sinking ships. As claimed by McBride, for daughters of narcissists, a breakup can cause a collapse that's equivalent to post-traumatic stress. A few years of dating and then breaking up can be destructive. McBride states, "They often think that maybe they won't find someone who cares about them for who they are."

The narcissistic parent has no intention of hurting the child; they don't even realize what they're doing. They are utterly blind to the fact that they are stigmatizing their children; it's a blind spot for the child as well. When a parent says something like *I'm so sorry your relationship didn't work out*, they think they're being empathetic. However, they never taught the child how to love or be loved, so how will such a statement stem from empathy or even be helpful on any level? Campbell reassures that "There's no magic solution, you have to be adult enough to realize that, and get the most out of what you can." Behary then advises that the best medicine for children of narcissists is having people to run interference—friends, other family members, or a personal mentor who can step in and mediate.

Campbell recommends, in addition to the adult child surrounding themself with loving friends, encouraging the parent when they are successful at being empathetic or caring by telling them that they made a wise parenting choice. Using their personality as leverage, they'll probably have the behavior reinforced that is needed in the long haul. Behary suggests another approach: holding the parent accountable. Narcissists dislike hearing about their faults and will usually become defensive when they're confronted with mistakes. Behary proposes that daughters set boundaries and accountability. She recommends using a script that affords the parent the benefit of the doubt: "I understand you care about me, but I am hurt when you do this." They are likely to say that they are only considering the well-being of the child, who must be prepared to politely reinforce their position by saying "Thank you, I appreciate your concern, but I'm only telling you how I feel." A parent may never have known that what they're doing hurts them, and that may be enough to get them to change their approach.

The only impossible journey is the one you never begin.

— Tony Robbins

*   *   *

McBride ultimately believes that the daughter of a narcissist has to determine if she wants to have civil contact with the parent, instead of the intrusive, compromising relationship she's been used to. Whatever the approach, their partner will need to be prepared to meet them. McBride urges preparing the partner to answer a torrent of questions and endure criticisms about education, job, plans, and so on. The objective is to prevent the partner from going away feeling judged. Following that, the couple can build a united front and provide support to implement clear boundaries.

The person grows up complying with the parent as if they were the only adult in the room and is not allowed to feel or have problems. They consistently have to struggle for a fraction of attention, as the parent is the only one allowed to have the concerns or feelings. Their emotions are the center of the room, and nobody else's emotions matter to them very much. The child often feels victimized; this stems from the fact that the parent's needs, wants, and experience are the only things that matter. Also, children of narcissists usually feel there's always something missing within them. They're constantly looking for their self...where is their self? Either one or both parents have encompassed them.

Traditionally, a narcissist will attract another narcissist: interestingly enough it is a perpetuating cycle of disease. The children grow up not knowing what their feelings mean. They have always encountered an environment where the parent's beliefs are the most important thing, and their feelings have taken a back seat, so the children feel like outcasts in their own families. They frequently sabotage their self to please those around them. They stop being interested in taking care of themselves because the child has understood that to get attention, affection—anything—they'll have to play the game of the parent. So, to fit into that distinct model, they've got to do whatever is right for the adult, not for themself. That means that they totally lose any sense of what is right for them and emerge as individuals into the adult world, in relationships, usually either wholly lost in terms of their own needs, or they become narcissistic in a bid to survive and in an effort to find a voice. The only way they know how to do that is by reflecting the parent.

The narcissistic parent will often mock the child for having feelings or interfere with the child's self-expression, so the youth will often feel like they are never heard and can never be seen. It is tormenting, and candidly, these individuals call themselves survivors, survivors of the narcissistic parent. It is very unpleasant and painful. As an adult, it is important to monitor that we are not at the mercy of any narcissistic impulses. We can shut down that part inside us with heightened awareness, being very present and in the moment, asking, *Am I reasonable in this debate? Or, am I overly demanding? Alternatively, am I in a relationship that is just like my parents'?*

If this tendency is detected, take note of this advice. Begin to write a journal, and as you notice everything around you, ask if you are narcissistic. Or are you currently in a relationship with a narcissist, or are you suffering from the consequences, the damaging effects in the form of depression, in the way of not knowing yourself, not knowing your voice, not knowing who you are, not knowing what it is you need and want in your relationships? Gradually begin to whisper your clear desires within you. Soon, those desires will become louder, and they'll do so in a more balanced and healthy way because of self-love, love for your parents and everyone. This is the actual journey of healing. Self-compassion, self-acknowledgment, and self-empathy are the true beginnings of healing. So, that is what I want you to work on. I want to say that I have much compassion for you. The capacity to empathize and have compassion for another person symbolizes a person evolving into mental, emotional, and spiritual health.

To give up on love is to choose a life that is less
human. To give up on love is to give up on life.

— Erwin McManus

Being in contact with yourself means that you face trouble-some truths and displeasing feelings. The only time you can progress is, when challenged by your demons, you take that as an opportunity to connect with yourself and deal with it the minute these feelings surface. You should be grateful to those who bring the worst out of you, as this is a chance to turn things around and improve. There's no other way to advance otherwise. This is the hardest thing to do. *Experience is what you get when you haven't got what you wanted.* Dr. Mohamud A. Verjee.

Spirituality is mainly about being authentic, hence being your-self. Enlightenment is the most exhaustive approach to being your-self, yet the most effective. There is always a place for meditation in spirituality, to guide you to become aware of yourself. In meditation, you focus on a certain point in your body. When you notice that you have drifted away from this point of focus, you gently return to it. By meditating, you learn to become mindful of what's happening in you and to stay present with that. You learn to stay in the moment and over time. This makes you tranquil, calm, relaxed, and ultimately more yourself.

* * *

CHAPTER 4:
MEDITATION, YOGA,
AND PRAYING

*If the ocean can calm itself, so can you. We
are both salt water mixed with air.*

— Nayyirah Waheed

Mastering Meditation

Many methods, therapies, and meditation practices can help people develop a sense of absolute happiness. The most effective path is through honest prayer to God through the exercise of holy religion. Prayer itself is a compelling way to amplify our insight of absolute happiness, but the action of distributing the knowledge acquired through spiritual practice also plays a significant role.

He who lights his neighbor's path lights his own way.

— Etnikas

The advantage of living a peaceful life with an intrinsic sense of happiness is becoming more and more acknowledged by science nowadays. The widespread benefits of the synchronization of mind, body, and spirit are now reinforced and honored across an extensive range of platforms. Spirituality is on a path to work in synergy with science, bringing traditional medicine together with ancient healing techniques, with a vision of having science unveil these techniques soon. Science and religion are not opposites and can be undoubtedly integrated. The research and exploration of mind-body states and infinite dimensions of consciousness can be part of a new spiritual and religious purpose, encompassing science and technology to become a unifying force for humankind.

> By time, indeed mankind is in loss. Except for those who
> have believed and done righteous deeds and advised
> each other to truth and advised each other to patience.

— Quran, CH103: V3.

The sacred plant medicine Ayahuasca is sometimes referred to as the *rope of death*. This means the death of negativity as a chance for the restoration of positive energy. It enables people to open their eyes to the majestic planet we live on, to celebrate our existence, and to be grateful. The ultimate goal of this plant medicine is to establish a connection between the individual, the universe, and God. This association sanctions us to recognize the value of living in harmony with, as opposed to dominance over, nature and people. *Apus* (a Peruvian word) are spirits that inhabit humans, have a protective duty and reside in peaks, glaciers, mountains, and hilltops. Their purpose is to serve all living beings and make sure they find happiness. In South America, the mountain called Aconcagua is the main *Apu*, located between Argentina and Chile.

The South American Inkari prophecy is a reference to the era of light and reawakening; this is where the wisdom of the ancient one is rediscovered. Spiritual philosophies from both the East and West recognize that we are in a new era, in which we are witnessing the emergence of light, love, and wisdom. This is called the Age of Aquarius in the East and as the Inkari Prophecy in the West. Spiritual academies tend to acknowledge that the energetic spiritual power has shifted from East to West, and the center of spiritual energy now dwells predominantly in South America and the Andes mountains. This region is considered to be a feminine energy center of the Earth. It becomes more evident as the reign of the energetic male center of the planet begins to subside. The *Apu* of the energetic male center of the world is called Sagarmatha and is also known as Mount Everest. There is something very compelling to the human spirit about mountains and their peaks. The highest peak in Africa is called Uhuru Peak on Mount Kilimanjaro. Uhuru means *freedom*, and one can only understand what it means to be free when you're on top of a mountain. In Africa, Iboga is the equivalent of Ayahuasca, and Syrian rue in the Middle East, and they all happen to grow near or on mountains. It seems like every plant medicine has its own effect reflecting the environment it lies in. One thing they all have in common, though, is that they heal mentally, physically, and spiritually, and they are incorporated into meditative states.

The most critical moment of any religious practice, as well as in our daily lives, is prayer. Prayer is a conversation with God where we are both speaking and listening in a state of love and respect. It is a form of meditation as well. It empowers us to make the right decisions and to attract the right situations to our daily lives. It allows us to advance our lives with an attitude of total gratefulness for both the positive and negative components of daily living. We learn to embrace the adverse circumstances because it is through this pain and suffering that we discover the way to happiness and liberation.

When you rise in the morning, give thanks for the light, for your life, for your strength. Give thanks for your food and the joy of living. If you see no reason to give thanks, the fault lies in yourself.

— Tecumseh

* * *

As in other ancient religions, the South American Incan religion holds sexuality in high honor. Sexuality in Incan beliefs is viewed to be the union of heaven and earth. To practice sacred sexuality, it is crucial that it is interlaced with love, transparency, and an awareness of preservation of one's sexual energy. Furthermore, it is recommended that sexual union be engaged in from a religious viewpoint. For the Incas, sexuality was regarded as a form of high-quality therapy. If practiced accurately, it could bring happiness as well as mental, physical, and spiritual prosperity. When the union was created correctly, it was believed that a couple could enter a trance of holy spirit or dharma.

Know that this union is a holy and pure thing when it is properly conducted in the proper time, and with the proper intention... God has created everything according to His wisdom, and has not created

things to be ugly or shameful... He created man and
woman, and created each and every organ and their
functions, and there is nothing degrading in this.

— Torah, Ramban, Igeret Hakodesh, Chapter 2.

If done incorrectly, however, it could bring unhappiness and suffering. It is necessary to remember that custom in sexuality can be severe as it can cripple the relations of true love and transparency. There's a reason why it's a highly revered practice in Islam as well: "He created you from a single soul, and from that soul He created his mate that he might dwell in serenity with her" Quran, CH7: V189. In Judaism it's also believed that "A husband and wife are one soul, separated only through their descent to this world. When they are married, they are reunited again" Torah, The Zohar, 191a. That's why we are advised to search for a mate very carefully, and it's always favorable to be able to find a person that matches your spiritual level. If you have already established a belief that God is a manifestation of everything, that praying and meditation brings you closer to God, to yourself, and humanity, then attract a match made in heaven, as it were, or your other lost half. It's considered a spiritual union celebrating in a twirling dance of bliss. Being able to connect with your energy center is, therefore, extremely important. Meditation is the stepping-stone in achieving this.

Meditation is an essential practice for self-realization. It requires sitting (or standing) straight and focusing on specific pressure points in your body—usually the belly, or it can be the nose, sensing the subtle sensations of breath through the nostrils. If you notice that you float or drift away from this point of concentration, you tenderly return to it. This practice in a steady approach helps with many details of your life. It makes you more conscious of the present moment—the here and now, magnifying the sense of time to face your current situations. It unfolds a deep level of concentration and awareness of the self and body, and it also balances energy and the chakras that will declutter the mental chatter in your head and make you calmer and more relaxed. This helps you become more open to yourself and the world and to be your natural self. People commonly meditate for fifteen to thirty minutes at a time, once or twice a day. It is preferable to meditate at least twenty minutes a day.

You can concentrate on the upper part of the belly, on the motion of the breath. Generally, this is the point used in Zen meditation. Alternatively, you can focus on the spot called the Dantian or Kath that is located one and a half thumb widths below the navel, two to three thumb widths inside of the body. Dantian originates in Chinese martial arts and qigong. It is an important energy center, which is located in the core of the body. Kath is traditionally used in the Diamond Approach and originates in Sufism.

Resist the urge to exclude surrounding distractions while focusing on your meditation point. It is all right to sense your body and embrace your feelings, as long as your meditation point is a component of what you are detecting. It is vital to sit straight and comfortably, with a firm sense of stability. Usually, people meditate sitting in a lotus position, with crossed legs resting on a cushion, or on their heels with the legs folded. Depending on your seated position, you can place your hands on your lap or your knees. You can set your hands in a specific position (a mudra). If you position them on your lap, keep your palms facing up and one on top of the other. Place your left hand underneath the right, its palm touching the back of the fingers of the right side. If you prefer to place your hands on your knees, let the backs of your hands rest on your knees. Lock the tips of the middle finger (or index finger) and the thumb. You can keep your eyes closed or look at the floor not too far ahead. If you choose to have your eyes open, make sure that the area in front of you is not too distracting, and meditate in a tranquil and dim space.

It is inevitable that thoughts surface. There is no problem with thoughts, except when there is a horde of thoughts that make it laborious to sense yourself and your situation, which is the case with many people. When you realize that you are thinking or fantasizing, gently and subtly return to your point of focus. Don't try to suppress thoughts, but restore focus.

The whole universe is composed of energy, and your body is no exception. Before modern science and technology, ancient wisdom recognized that all living beings conveyed a life force within them. They described the centers of energy that move inside of us, as the seven chakras. Chakra is an old Sanskrit term that translates to *wheel*.

Peace. It doesn't mean to be in a place where there is no noise, trouble or hard work. It means to be in the midst of those things and still be calm in your heart.

— Anonymous

*   *   *

This potent life force, or prana, that circulates inside of you is spinning and rotating. This spinning energy has seven centers in your body, springing into life at the base of your spine and running up to the top of your head. In a physically (and mentally) healthy, balanced person, the seven chakras provide precisely the exact amount of energy to every boundary of your body, mind, and spirit. Nevertheless, if one of your chakras is too open and spinning too quickly, or if it is blocked and moving slowly, your health will be adversely affected. By learning about the seven chakras, you can become in tune with the connate energy cycles in your body. You can utilize this knowledge to connect physical, emotional, and spiritual disparity with the chakras that emancipate and bring balance, thus living healthily.

*　*　*

There's More to Yoga

*Yoga is a way of moving into stillness in order
to experience the truth of who you are.*

— Erich Schiffman

If you're a spirited yoga practitioner, you've probably perceived some of the benefits that yoga encompasses—maybe improved sleep or getting sick less often or merely being more relaxed and mentally at ease. However, if you lecture a novice about the benefits of yoga, you might find that lines like *It increases the flow of prana* or *It brings the energy up your spine* fall on deaf or cynical ears. As it presents itself, science is starting to dispense some concrete evidence as to how yoga works to refine health, alleviate aches and pains, and mitigate sickness. Once you infer the knowledge, you'll have even more incentive to step onto a mat, and you probably won't feel so unprepared the next time someone asks for unadulterated proof.

For starters, improved flexibility is the most apparent and most palpable virtues of yoga. In your first class, you probably won't be able to reach your toes, never mind do a backbend. Nonetheless, if you stick with it, you'll notice a progressive loosening, and over the long haul, unusual poses will seem possible. Chances are you'll observe that aches and pains start to melt away, and that's no coincidence. Tight hips can exhaust the knee joint due to the erroneous alignment of the shinbones and thighs. Stiff hamstrings can result in a flattened lumbar spine, which can cause back pain. Besides, inflexibility in muscles and connective tissue can bring about poor posture. Your head is like a ball—round, large, and heavy. When it's balanced straight atop an upright spine, it requires much less effort for your back and neck muscles to hold it up. Move it a tad forward, and you start to overextend those muscles. Carry that forward-leaning ball for twelve hours a day, and it's no wonder you feel drained. Fatigue might not be your only concern: poor posture can also cause back, neck, muscle, and joint problems. As you slump, your body may compensate by flattening the standard inward curves in your neck and lower back. This can cause degenerative arthritis of the spine over time or even abruptly.

Spinal disks are the shock absorbers between the vertebrae that can compress and herniate nerves—thirst movement. That's hardly the way they get nutrients. If you have an even-handed asana practice with lots of backbends, forward bends, and twists, you'll help keep your disks agile. Advanced yogis can hold sway over their bodies in remarkable ways, many of which are moderated by the nervous system. Physicians have observed yogis who could prompt unusual heart rhythms, generate unusual brain-wave patterns, use a meditation technique, and raise the temperature of their hands by nine degrees Celsius. If yoga can help to do that, perhaps you could learn to enrich blood flow to your pelvis if you're attempting to get pregnant, or coax yourself into relaxation when you're facing difficulty in falling asleep. Yoga gets your blood flowing. More precisely, the relaxation calisthenics you acquire in yoga can assist your circulation, specifically in your hands and feet. Yoga also helps transport more oxygen to your cells, which operate better as a result. Twisting poses are known to press out venous blood from internal organs and give way to oxygenated blood flowing in as soon as the twist is released.

> *Surround yourself with more people who remind*
> *you that waking up this morning was the first*
> *blessing of that day and balancing on two hands*
> *(or feet) is a privilege we take for granted.*

— Hana Elleithy

* * *

Inverted poses, such as the handstand, headstand, and shoulder stand, boost venous blood from the pelvis and legs to flow back to the heart, so it's pumped to the lungs and become freshly oxygenated. This can be a relief if you suffer from swelling in your legs due to heart or kidney problems. Moreover, yoga contributes to heightening levels of hemoglobin and red blood cells, which transfer oxygen to the tissues.

When you habitually get your heart rate to the aerobic span, you lower the risk of heart attacks and can mitigate depression. Although not all yoga is aerobic, if you carry out the stretches vigorously or take flow or Ashtanga classes, it can raise your heart rate to the aerobic range. However, even yoga movements that don't raise your heart rate can still improve cardiovascular conditioning. Studies have discovered that yoga reduces the resting heart rate, strengthens endurance, and can enhance your maximum uptake of oxygen during practice—all indications of improved aerobic conditioning. One study suggested that subjects who were taught only pranayama could do more exercise with less oxygen. Yogis have a propensity to take fewer breaths of larger volume, which is both efficient and more calming. A study published in the British medical journal *The Lancet* in 1999 taught a yogic technique known as *complete breathing* to people with lung complications ascribed to congestive heart failure. A month later, their average respiratory rate went down from 13.4 breaths per minute to 7.6. In the interim, their workout capacity notably increased, as did the oxygen saturation in their blood. Moreover, yoga has been shown to improve an assortment of measures related to lung function, comprising the apex volume of breathing and the efficiency of the exhalation. Yoga also prompts breathing through the nose, which helps purify the air, warms and humidifies the passage (cold, dry air is more likely to stir up an asthma attack in sensitive people), and removes grime and other impurities you'd rather not inhale into your lungs.

You might benefit from yoga as well if you've got a high blood pressure. Two studies of individuals with hypertension, published in *The Lancet*, contrasted the effects of Savasana (corpse pose) with merely lying on a couch. Three months later, Savasana was associated with a twenty-six-point decrease in systolic blood pressure and a fifteen-point reduction in diastolic pressure. Strong muscles do more than look good. They also shield us from situations like arthritis and back pain and help prevent falls in seniors. So, when you build up strength through yoga, you balance it with flexibility.

The nature of yoga is to shine the light of awareness into the darkest corners of the body.

— Jason Crandell

* * *

You move your organs around when you contract and stretch the muscles when coming in and out of yoga postures. You also surge the drainage of lymph, a thick fluid rich in immune cells. This supports the lymphatic system fighting infection, battling cancerous cells, and disposing of the toxic waste products of cellular functioning. Furthermore, yoga lowers cortisol levels. Usually, the adrenal glands secrete cortisol in retaliation to a dire crisis, which provisionally boosts the immune function. If your cortisol levels remain high even after the stressing event, they can jeopardize the immune system. Provisional growth of cortisol levels helps with long-term memory, but chronically high levels sabotage memory and may lead to lasting alterations in the brain.

Additionally, imprudent levels of cortisol have been linked with severe depression, osteoporosis (it draws out calcium and other minerals from bones and obstructs the foundation of new bones), insulin resistance, and high blood pressure. High cortisol levels result in what researchers call food-seeking behavior (the kind that impels you to eat when you're sad, angry, or stressed). The body takes those extra calories and circulates them as fat, causing weight gain and increased risk of diabetes and heart attack.

It's reported that weight-bearing practices strengthen bones and help fend off osteoporosis. Many postures in yoga demand that you lift your weight, like downward- and upward-facing dog for instance, help strengthen the arm bones, which are especially suscep-tible to osteoporotic fractures. In a study administered at California State University, Los Angeles, yoga practice amplified bone density in the vertebrae. Yoga's ability to lower stress-hormone cortisol lev-els may assist in keeping the required calcium in the bones. Each time you perform yoga, you carry your joints through a full range of motion. This may impede degenerative arthritis or lighten disability by squeezing and soaking cartilages, as it were, that generally aren't utilized. Joint cartilage is comparable to a sponge: it acquires fresh nutrients only when the fluid is squeezed out, and a recently devel-oped supply can be soaked up. Without real sustenance, mistreated areas of cartilage can at some point wear out, exposing the masked bone like worn-out brake pads.

The battle of yoga is with the body and with the ego.
You must conquer your ego, or small self, so that you
can let your soul, your big Self, be victorious.

— B. K. S. Iyengar

* * *

As you read all the different ways yoga improves your health, you will have probably noticed much overlap. That's because they're immensely interlaced. Change your posture, and you impact the way you breathe. Change your breathing, and you influence your nervous system. This is one of the appreciable lessons of yoga:

everything is connected—your hip bone to your anklebone, your anklebone to you, you to society, society to the world. This interconnection is crucial to comprehending yoga. This synergy may be the most important mechanism of all that yoga heals. The fundamentals of yoga—asana, pranayama, and meditation—act to ameliorate your health, but there's more in the yoga magic box. You may want to consider chanting as well. Chanting tends to extend exhalation, which sways the balance in the direction of the parasympathetic nervous system. When performed in a group setting, chanting can be an unusually powerful physical and emotional experience. A study from Sweden's Karolinska Institute presents that humming sounds—like those made while incanting *om*—open the sinuses and expedites drainage. We must also consider the emotional implications of yoga as well as the physical ones. If you are feeling down, sit in the lotus position. Better still, rise to a backbend or take off majestically into a king dancer pose. While it's not as easy as it may seem, one study found that a regular yoga exercise improved depression and led to a remarkable rise in serotonin levels and a fall in the levels of monoamine oxidase (the enzyme that breaks down neurotransmitters) as well as cortisol. Dr. Richard Davidson at the University of Wisconsin discovered an amplified activity in the left prefrontal cortex in meditators' brains, a finding that has been connected to higher levels of happiness and enhanced immune function. More noticeable left-sided amplification was detected in dedicated, long-term practitioners.

The rhythm of the body, the melody of the mind and
harmony of the soul create the symphony of life.

— B. K. S. Iyengar

* * *

Yoga subdues the shifts of the mind, as stated by Patanjali's Yoga Sutra. In other words, it sedates the mental loops of frustration, resentment, anger, fear, regret, and desire created by the ego that can result in stress. Stress is correlated to so many health problems—migraines, insomnia, high blood pressure, and heart attacks—that, if you learn to silence your mind, you'll be likely to live longer and healthier. Yoga inspires you to relax, steady your breath, and focus on the now, altering the balance from the sympathetic nervous system (fight-or-flight response) to the parasympathetic nervous system. The outcome is calming and recuperative; it modulates breathing and heart rates, lowers blood pressure, and builds up blood flow to the intestines and reproductive organs—incorporating what Dr. Herbert Benson regards as the relaxation response. Irritable bowel syndrome, ulcers, constipation, all of these can be worsened by stress. So, if you stress less often, you'll eventually suffer less.

Yoga also soothes constipation—and theoretically speaking lowers the risk of colon cancer—because moving the body catalyzes the transport of food and waste products quickly through the bowels. Moreover, even though it has not been scientifically proven, yogis suppose that twisting poses may be favorable in getting waste to move through the system. Yoga can ease your physical suffering in a variety of ways. According to several studies, asana, meditation, or both combined lowered pain in people with arthritis, back pain, carpal tunnel syndrome, fibromyalgia, and other chronic conditions. When you relieve your pain, your mood gets better, and you're more likely to be active. Asana and pranayama in all probability improve the immune function; however, meditation has the strongest scientific evidence favoring it in this regard.

Moreover, yoga reduces blood sugar and LDL ("bad") cholesterol and increases HDL ("good") cholesterol. In people with diabetes, yoga has been discovered to reduce their blood sugar in various ways: by lowering cortisol as well as adrenaline levels, promoting weight loss, and advancing sensitivity to the impacts of insulin. If you get your blood-sugar levels down, you decrease the risk of diabetic complexities such as heart attack, kidney failure, and blindness. Therefore, it's highly desirable to stretch more and eat less—that's the dictum of many yogis. Yoga helps on both ends. Regular exercise gets you burning calories, and the spiritual and emotional aspects of the practice may energize you to confront any eating and weight problems on a deeper level. It encourages you to become a more conscious eater. Kriyas, or cleansing exercises, are another component of yoga. They include rapid-breathing exercises and internal cleansing of the intestines. If you envision an image in your mind, as you do in yoga nidra for example, you can exert change in your body. Several studies in Sweden have uncovered that guided imagery reduced pain, the frequency of headaches, and an enriched quality of life for individuals with cancer or HIV. Proper yoga guidance can do miracles for your health. Exceptional instructors undertake more than posture guidance. They can fine-tune your stance, assess when you should go more in depth in poses or transition back, provide harsh truths with compassion, help you relax, and personalize your practice, lifestyle, and diet. A respectful relationship with a yoga instructor goes a long way toward boosting your health.

Karma yoga (service to others) is built into the yogic philosophy. While you may not be inclined to serve others, your health might improve if you do so. A study at the University of Michigan disclosed that seniors who volunteered around an hour a week were three times more likely to be alive seven years later. Community service can impart meaning to your life, and your issues may not seem so discouraging when you see what other people are going through. Most patients are passive receivers of care in conventional medicine. In yoga, it's what you do for your betterment that matters. Yoga gives you the gadgets to help you change, and you might begin to feel better from the first time you practice. You may also realize that the more you commit to exercising, the more you benefit in three main things: you become immersed in your care, you discover that your participation gives you the power to carry out change, and observing that you can carry out reform, you are empowered and filled to the brim with hope. Also, hope itself can be healing, as it supports immense changes in your life. That might be its most significant strength. Tapas, the Sanskrit term for *heat*, is the fire, the flair that fuels yoga training and that consistent practice builds up. The tapas you bring into being can be extended to the rest of your life to vanquish stasis and dysfunctional habits.

You may find that without making a discrete effort to change things, you begin eating better, exercising more, quit smoking after years of failed attempts, or even sleep better: studies indicate that another by-product of a consistent yoga practice is better-quality sleep, which means you'll be less fatigued and stressed. Stimulation is excellent, but too much of it taxes the nervous system. Yoga can provide relief from the scuttle and scramble of modern life. Restorative asana, yoga nidra (guided relaxation), Savasana, pranayama, and meditation promote pratyahara, a tuning inward into your senses, which translate into downtime for the nervous system.

Most humans are never fully present in the now, because
unconsciously they believe that the next moment

must be more important than this one. But then you
miss your whole life, which is never not now.

— Eckhart Tolle

* * *

An essential component of yoga is focusing on the present moment. Studies have uncovered that regular yoga exercise enhances coordination, memory, response time, and even IQ scores. People familiar with transcendental meditation verify the ability to solve problems, acquire and remember information more easily—probably since they're less distracted by their thoughts, which tend to loop endlessly. Regular practice distends proprioception—the ability to intuitively know what your body is doing and where it is in space—and hence improves balance. People with poor posture or dysfunctional movement habits usually have deficiencies in proprioception. Proper balance could mean fewer falls due to imbalance. For the elderly, this could mean more independence and less chance of being forced into a nursing home. For the younger crowd, postures like tree pose can make us less wobbly on and off the mat.

The body benefits from movement, and
the mind benefits from stillness.

— Sakyong Mipham

* * *

Yoga and meditation build awareness. So, the more conscious you are, the simpler it is to break free of destructive emotions like rage. Studies indicate that chronic anger and malevolence are as strongly related to heart attacks as smoking, diabetes, and high levels of cholesterol. Yoga appears to shrink anger by increasing feelings of compassion and interconnection and by calming the nervous system and the mind. It also increases your ability to snap out of the present drama in your life and to remain steadfast in the face of disturbing events. You can still react swiftly when you need to—and there's evidence that yoga increases reaction time—but you can take control of that split second to choose a more thoughtful approach, minimizing suffering for yourself and others. Love may not conquer all, but it does help in healing. Cultivating the emotional support of friends, family, lovers, and community has been substantiated by studies repeatedly to refine health and healing. Regular yoga helps develop friendliness, compassion, and outward composure. Aligned with yogic philosophy's importance on avoiding harm to others, telling the truth, and consuming only what you need, this may ameliorate many of your relationships. Many of us suffer from persistent low self-esteem. If managed negatively, we can end up taking drugs, binge eating, working too hard or too little, promiscuity, laziness, and the compromising of our health mentally, physically, and spiritually.

On the other hand, by practicing yoga you'll sense a positive approach, initially in momentary glimpses but later in longer-lasting instances, and will feel that you're worthwhile or even a manifestation of the divine. If you regularly perform with the intention of self-introspection and betterment—not just as a replacement for an aerobics class or CrossFit complimentary stretches—you can access an unknown side of yourself. You'll experience gratitude, forgiveness, feelings of empathy, and most importantly a sense that you are part of something much bigger.

Yoga is not a work-out, it is a work-in. And this is the
point of spiritual practice; to make us teachable; to open
up our hearts and focus our awareness so that we can
know what we already know and be who we already are.

— Rolf Gates

*   *   *

While better health is only one constituent of spirituality, it's often a by-product as well, as reported by scientific studies. Believing you will get better can compel you to become better. Unfortunately, many traditional scientists trust that if something works by evoking the placebo effect, it doesn't count as an endorsed scientific law. Most patients want to get well, so if chanting a mantra enables healing, even if it's a placebo effect, why not do it then? If your medicine drawer is similar to a pharmacy, maybe it's time to try yoga. There is evidence of people with asthma, high blood pressure, type 2 diabetes, and OCD who tried yoga and were able reduce their dosage of medications and in some cases get off them completely. The advantages of taking fewer drugs? You are probably less likely to undergo the side effects and risk dangerous drug interactions.

*   *   *

What Is Praying All About?

Let there be spaces in your togetherness and let the
winds of the heavens dance between you. Love one

another but make not a bond of love: let it rather be
a moving sea between the shores of your souls.

— Kahlil Gibran

Praying is the combination of meditation in its spiritual form and yoga in its physical and mental form. It is the fastest way to connect with spirit. There are many ways to communicate with God of course, but there is a reason why it's called Salat as in Selah or *connection*. It's a means of communicating with the divine source and moving toward the light and truth. Of course, many people pray fast and claim they have done their duty. It's not about ticking a requirement off a checklist; praying or meditating should be done in a holy and divine way that touches your soul every single time. I am striving to understand the science behind the indispensable movements and the wisdom behind going through it during specific times of the day. It's a matter of time until all the reasons unfold scientifically.

Prayers are putting oneself in the hand of God. The reason Islam (*surrender*) requires an individual to offer Salat five times a day (if they are mentally and physically capable of doing so in any capacity) is for constant remembrance for their true essence and connection to the source or the divine. It is an essential pillar for surrendering and a significant practice that draws you out of life's distractions to remind you of who you indeed are. To some practitioners (those who are not spiritual in their core and usually follow religion blindly without making any effort to understand its implications), Salat is a religious requirement and nothing else. For others, it is a sacrifice they make for God to express gratefulness for the blessings and the air we breathe in, as well as exhibiting humility of our being compared to the wholeness and power of the universe;

time is sacrificed for His remembrance in return. Or they may see it as a way to draw themselves closer to the source every day or to find refuge from every challenge that life throws at them.

> *Gratitude unlocks the fullness of life. It turns what we have into enough, and more. It turns denial into acceptance, chaos into order, confusion to clarity.*

— Melody Beattie

* * *

While Salat does have many obvious spiritual benefits, I want to draw attention to a handful that are not usually brought to mind or acknowledged. Everyone finds motivation or inspiration in a variety of ways; hopefully, these less popular benefits of Salat will help us appreciate more about its splendor. Let's keep in mind that praying is a form of meditation. Mindfulness meditation is a huge craze these days. There are guided practices on social media, sessions held on college campuses, and so on. Research has proven that mindfulness meditation can assist people to become more relaxed and conscientious. Salat is an almost identical form of meditation. It invites us to empty our minds of noises and rambling thoughts and to unwind our bodies. Amid our busy lives, meditation may be challenging to repeat for long periods, but Salat typically takes only five to ten minutes per prayer. In mindfulness meditation, people are advised to concentrate on their breathing or physical bodies. In Salat, the focus is only on the divine source of existence. Praying also stretches our bodies in ways similar to some yoga poses, such as the standing half-forward bend and the child's pose. We'll talk in depth later regarding the benefits of prayerful movements and its commonalities with yoga poses. For individuals with mental struggles such as depression and anxiety, Salat can be a call for relief. Even if someone does not have any ailments, it can help relax their mind and body. It removes us from the hustle-and-bustle of daily life and helps us reconnect our soul with its creator.

> *It really boils down to this: that all life is interrelated.*
> *We are all caught in an inescapable network of*
> *mutuality, tied into a single garment of destiny.*
> *Whatever affects one destiny affects all indirectly.*

— Martin Luther King Jr.

*   *   *

Prayers periodically also teach time management. There is always a multitude of things to do, and never enough time. Right? Time management helps a lot but is easier said than done. We don't realize how much time we have in a day until we start scheduling it in an organized manner. Salat is a simple, natural way to compartmentalize our time throughout any day by making us stop, bring awareness to the time of day, step back and meditate in serenity, then go back to what we're doing in a time-structured way. The fact that the prayers are spread throughout the day illustrates that no matter how busy the day is, we always have time to remember our divine source. Similarly, we can use the prayer timings to organize our tasks and errands on our to-do list which we might otherwise have thought we didn't have the time for.

The following benefit handles a common problem. Salat reveals to us what's preoccupying our mind and heart. This is a thorny one to acknowledge, and the tendency is to resist. During Salat, it's common to remember something unexpectedly that we otherwise couldn't recall: a catchy song abruptly plays in your head, or thinking of how we should have reacted or responded to a person. Likewise, all the things we need to do and what we're going to do right after praying can arise only during the practice, like the upcoming season finale of our favorite show, or fantasizing about a loved one or the person we have a crush on. The reason this is noteworthy is that it unveils what our mind and heart are prioritizing over God at that moment. It's a natural human frailty to be distracted during Salat, but we should always try to work on it. Meditation helps to reroute our focus and attention on to breathing, and it coerces us to shift our thoughts from distractions to connection to our inner force.

Additionally, prayers can connect us to others. It demonstrates the beauty of Islam and the connection it offers with God. While it's usually a private deed, the reason it's preferable to pray in groups is to show the power of uniformity, how a handful, hundreds, or even thousands of people can come together to perform synchronized movements and voice their intentions in gratitude. It's delivered in unity such that it does not discriminate between a laborer and a president standing shoulder to shoulder as equals, affirming that only God is great. Finally, Salat connects us to our source of love and gets us back on track. It can calm us down, without fail, when angry, sad, or just overreacting. It's a reminder that we are all one, and there is nothing worth endlessly dwelling on.

In his book, *Zaad al-Ma'aad*, Ibn al-Qayyim states in his discussion of medicines and nutrition "God the Exalted has said: 'And seek help in patience and Salat [prayer] and truly it is extremely heavy and hard except for Al-Khashi'un'" [i.e., the true believers who connect with full submission] Quran, CH2: V45. "Moreover, He has said: 'O you who believe! Seek help in patience and Salat [prayer]. Truly! Allah is with As-Sabirin [the patient ones]'" Quran, CH2: V153. "Also, He, the Exalted One, has stated: 'And gracefully enjoin Salat [the prayer] on your family, and be patient in offering them [prayers]'" Quran, CH20: V132.

Furthermore, it is reported that the Messenger of God, Muhammad (Peace Be Upon Him), used to hasten to prayer whenever a matter disturbed him. In the earlier days, people turned to prayers for healing most ailments before seeking out other ways of dealing with them. Prayer is a practice that causes us to receive nourishment that safeguards our physical (makes the limbs active, enhancing physical flexibility), mental (keeping negative energy at bay through meditative states), and spiritual health (reenergizing the heart and soul by getting rid of laziness). Overall it has an astonishing effect on the health of the body and spirit, in strengthening them and expelling negativity.

Prayer allows the believer to refine and elevate their spirituality and enrich the soul's right to love the creator and his creations (us). The importance of prayer is consistently conveyed in the Quran and was also emphasized by the Prophet Muhammad (PBUH): "Know that among your duties, prayer is foremost." Praying five times a day is considered vital to attaining health and success in this life and the hereafter. It's a perpetual reminder of the essence of our creation and pledges a direct connection to the creator, who linked health, success, and pleasure to humility in prayer. Praying also draws attention to the proximity between spirituality, science, and daily life. At some point, life will direct us to unite ourselves with our creator. It is an opportunity for remembrance that we are here to unite, not further divide. Interrupting daily activities promotes the realization of this concept. Through prayer, a believer acquires spiritual awareness that he takes with him throughout all of life's endeavors.

Prayer purifies the heart, and indeed, through practicing it, a believer eventually fulfills spiritual devotion and moral elevation. Salat not only gives a deep connection with the One, but in it, patience, sincerity, and humility are learned. It also provides a vehicle for remorse and allows our unconscious to heal by going through our feelings with no judgments. This is presented through the saying of the Prophet Muhammad (PBUH): "'If a person had a stream outside his door and he bathed in it five times a day, do you think he would have any dirt left on him?' The people said, 'No filth would remain on him whatsoever.' The Prophet (peace be upon him) then said, 'That is like the five daily prayers: Allah wipes away the sins by them.'" (From the Hadeeth collections of Al-Bukhari) It is through sincere prayers that one indeed finds inner peace and self-actualization.

* * *

Ablution with Clean Water

The typical physical movements of prayers have been beautifully consolidated with spiritual exercise, resulting in many unexpected health benefits. Salat is the spiritual prescription from our source for better health and fitness to those who practice it regularly. Thus, it is a natural way to stay healthy. Before praying, one has to go through ablution with water, where one rinses their hands, arms, face, and feet to ward off germs from the body and thus promote good health. It stimulates active biological areas similar to Chinese reflexology, which has beneficial therapeutic impacts on the hands, face, and feet.

Additionally, it helps to relax the nervous system and eases tension, stress, and anxiety. Washing our hands five times a day before Salat is an effective way to repel germs from the body. Gargling during ablution is crucial as it helps to remove bacteria, allergens, and dust particles. It reduces viral respiratory infections and ensures a diminution in bad breath as well. Nose cleansing during ablution removes clouds of dust and contaminated matter, and doing this with water helps to minimize infections such as flu, sinusitis, the common cold, and chest infections. It also helps overcome nasal congestion and clear sticky matter in the nose. Face washing is mainly for refreshing as well as enhancing the facial complexion and skin tone. It reduces the effect of oily skin and hinders the growth of acne and wrinkles. Ear cleaning helps to prevent wax accumulation. Cleaning both ears with wet fingers five times a day is also good to get rid of dust and germs from the outer ears.

Finally, washing the feet helps to remove specks of dirt and prevent fungus. The act of washing your feet imitates acupressure when fingers pass through the bottom region of the toes. Rubbing the toes is especially beneficial for diabetes, and many accu points are present in the upper and lower parts of the toes so pressing these during ablution may help ease soreness in the back, arthritic joints, and so on.

There's a voice that doesn't use words. Listen.

— Rumi

* * *

Praying and Meditation

Meditating is highly beneficial to activate all the seven chakras as per the yogic philosophy. There is a high correlation between praying and meditation. Meditation revitalizes the mechanism of body and mind. It is a refreshing routine and also a cost-effective solution for promptly detecting the very root cause of diseases. It also restores harmony among an assortment of lifestyle elements: physical, social, emotional, spiritual, mental, and psychological. The notion of meditation is to relish and cherish life with invigorating excitement. The process provides psychological and emotional well-being. Being a drugless therapy, it augments the sustainable and functional ability of the body. The same applies to Salat. Meditation and praying are indeed a substitute for stress and promote a disease-free personality. Praying is the most elegant form of meditation or Dhyan; from a yogic point of view this is when an individual unilaterally surrenders to the divine source. Meditation is described as the uninterrupted flow of mind toward a specific focus point. Praying is one of the best tension-reliever modalities and is the perfect example of meditation where the performer focuses only on one thing. Thus, praying yields the utmost satisfaction and peace of mind besides an enhanced concentration and reduced levels of depression.

Praying and Yoga

Prayers are not just practices that an individual performs; the benefits of prayers are evident in the physical and spiritual aspects of the entire practice. Prayers consist of several movements and postures. It includes sets of rakaat, and each set of rakaa consists of a series of seven postures or poses. For example, before sunrise, two rakaat or fourteen poses should be carried out. Thus, a person who performs the five acts of prayers every day is under obligation to perform 119 poses per day, that is 3,750 poses per month, and approximately 42,840 postures per year. Prophet Muhammad (PBUH) said "There is a cure in prayers."

It's vital for the individual before starting prayers to have clear intentions of surrender and gratitude, along with being personally clean in terms of hygiene and clothes. God mentions love toward those who purify themselves (physically and spiritually): "Truly, Allah loves those who turn into him in repentance, and He loves those who purify themselves." Quran, CH2: V222.

For centuries, prayers that are composed of different postures and movements performed during Salat afford followers with many physical, mental, and spiritual benefits. Many yoga poses are similar to those which Muslims perform during Salat, and medical researchers have discovered that patients who do those simple movements improve their overall health.

Although many of the terms used by yogis might sound somewhat unfamiliar, understanding some of the states may explain the poses. In the research reported by Raof Ahmad Bhat, titled *Unity of Health through Yoga and Islamic Prayer "Salah,"* he describes how the yoga postures are linked to Salat more than we think. Most of the postures performed during Muslim prayers are very similar to yoga poses. When all the poses are performed successively, they activate what yogis refer to as chakras or the energy fields in the human body. Chakras can be interpreted as how our feeling sense operates and functions. Our bodies respond and become more aware when they're touched throughout the different movements. The main yoga similarities to postures done by Muslims during their daily prayers include the following.

Meditation in Yoga

Yoga International describes meditation or Dhyan, from a yogic point of view, thus: "The mind is clear, relaxed, and inwardly focused. When you meditate, you are fully awake and alert, but your mind is not focused on the external world or the events taking place around you." Meditation lowers stress, which can enhance sleep and mood and boosts the metabolic and immune systems. This is essentially why meditating throughout the day, whether it's before you sleep, after lunch, or when you wake up, is beneficial.

Meditation in Prayers

During prayer, a Muslim must devote himself and surrender entirely to the divine source. It's a meeting between a spirit and his creator; hence, he should focus only on the divine. A Muslim is required to focus and leave out all life distractions and connect with God during that time. Prayers allow the person to feel that God is taking care of everything, instilling inner peace that promotes calmness and serenity.

Intentions of Yoga

The term *namaste* means *I bow to you* or *Bow me you*. Yogis place the hands together on the heart chakra to enlarge the flow of divine love, bowing the head, closing the eyes, and then bringing the hands down to the heart as a way to surrender to the divine in the heart. Namaste is regarded as a form of greeting from one person to another. The standing position of namaste enhances body posture and helps in strengthening the muscles around the spine. With it, the yogi can also plant an intention, seek wisdom, or show gratitude.

Moreover, yoga helps in building muscles without the need to do high-intensity workouts, thus improving metabolism and blood flow. The range of motions that are included in many yoga poses improve balance and flexibility. The muscle stretching enables the muscles to work more efficiently.

Intentions of Prayers

A person in prayer starts with the Takbir *Allah Akbar* meaning *God is the greatest,* while standing straight with both hands placed over the heart to commence Salat. Certain Quranic verses are recited at the start of each rakaa, such as "Guide us to the righteous path," Quran, CH1: V6, paved with good intentions, gratitude, and wisdom-seeking. The standing posture in prayer secures a straightened back and improves the person's overall posture by allowing proper blood flow to the lower part of the body. According to Bhat, when commencing Salat, the position helps in controlling "the awareness of self in the world and controls the health of the muscular system, skin, intestines, liver, gall bladder and eyes." It is also useful in strengthening the leg muscles. When the person spreads open their hands for prayer and intentions, the heart chakra gets activated. As mentioned, this is the center of love, harmony, and peaceful feelings, which assists the heart, lungs, immune system, and circulatory system health. Prayers require the movement of the body throughout the Salat performance; hence, it promotes physical activity and helps in stretching and activating several muscles, increasing flexibility and supporting a toned physique.

Half-standing Forward Fold in Yoga

Ardha Uttanasana is a half-standing forward fold. This yoga pose intensifies the link between breathing and movement, which quiets and relaxes the mind. Both Ruku' and Ardha Uttanasana help in strengthening the lower back (the core) and the spine, which improves the body posture. A regular, robust stretch of the muscles of the lower back helps in easing back pain in the long run. It also adds pressure to the abdomen, which provides relief for constipation and peristaltic movements, as well as toning the abdomen muscles.

Half-standing Forward Fold (Ruku') in Prayers

Ruku' is the half-standing forward bending position in prayers. It is also a humbling movement of bowing down to a supreme presence, letting go of one's pride, and submitting to that which requires work on the ego. The Prophet Muhammad (PBUH) advised to bow calmly and to get up only when the body has come to ease. Doing Ruku' correctly helps to gage backache and vertebral column–related diseases.

Child Pose in Yoga

In yoga, child pose is called Balasana. This is a familiar stretching pose that many execute in their daily routine. It helps in relieving the pain and tension in the lower back, shoulders, and chest. According to the research study done by Bhat, this pose is said to "activate the 'crown chakra' which is related to a person's spiritual connection with the universe around them and their enthusiasm for spiritual pursuits. This nerve pathway is also correlated to the health of the brain and pineal gland. Its healthy function balances one's interior and exterior energies."

Child Pose (Sujjod) in Prayers

The most crucial part of prayers is the Sujjod; this is when the forehead touches the ground. It is stated in a Hadith that this is the position where the person is nearest to his creator. Abu Huraira reports that the Messenger said "The nearest a believer comes to his Lord is when he is prostrating himself, so make supplication (in this state)." Sahih Al-Bukhari. This position allows smooth and increased blood flow to the brain. The posture of Sujjod and Balasana prevents the belly from accumulating more fats. The forehead on the ground as well as the knees and feet add pressure on the abdominal muscles, lower back, and core, making them much stronger. It's also an incredibly humbling pose that brings your brain and pineal gland (the sanctuary of your spirit's creation) closest to the earth or ground. Sujjod is very beneficial in the functioning of the brain, lungs, body muscles, joints, and vertebral column. It lowers the chances of brain hemorrhage and headaches with a steady blood flow to the head. While performing it, the toes are experiencing acupressure, which is excellent for body-ache resolution.

Kneeling in Yoga

Vajrasana is used by yogis to describe kneeling. It is suitable for digestion and keeps the spine firm and erect. It is best to do this pose after eating for maximum benefit. It helps in easing constipation, fighting stomach disease, and increasing the body's circulation. The pose also helps in calming the mind, which causes the body to relax. Moreover, it contributes to relieving the knee and ankle joints, as well as toning the hip, calf, and thigh muscles.

Kneeling (Julus) in Prayers

One of the main postures during prayers is the Julus, this is where a person recites the testification and bear to the Oneness of the creator and the apostleship of his revered Messenger. This posture involves sitting on both thighs, knees, and ankles and helps in curing joint pains and even assists in digestion by coercing stomach content downwards. It is beneficial for digestion and makes the spine firm and erect.

Salaam or Neck Yoga

Salaam is an exemplary form of neck and upper vertebra exercise. Prayer Salaam is the Griva-sakti-vikasaka (strengthening the neck) of yogic Sukshma Vyayama, which helps loosen the neck joints and encourages the shoulder and upper back muscles to relax. Salaam helps to refresh the nerves passing through the neck, thus useful in cases of headache or migraine.

* * *

Customary Salat involves a variety of physical movements and postures, which have been scientifically proven to have medical and health benefits. Even though people generally perform their daily prayers out of spirituality, modern science has shed light on the physical health benefits of Salat as well. The different positions during it help in improving the overall blood flow in the body, whether it's too high or too low in a particular region. In such cases, the Salat movements help in regulating the flow to all parts. During the Ruku' position, for example, blood flow is controlled in the upper body; during kneeling, the blood flow is managed in the lower body.

According to Bhat, Salat also helps in digestion. It improves liver functions and relaxes the intestines, which in turn promotes bowel movement. It can also alleviate some cases of constipation and change habits of overeating. The position of the body during prostration and bowing helps open up and ease the joints. Regular use of the bones preserves their health and functionality.

Moreover, the position of the Ruku' helps in alleviating pain in the lower back by relaxing the ligaments and muscles (similar to yoga). It also helps ease the pain in the spinal cord and hip joints. Through the vertebral relaxation, backache and vertebral illnesses can also be avoided. The Salat overall relaxes the shoulder joints, elbows, knees, ankles, and hips.

In essence, Salat is also a form of exercise, and it increases a person's metabolism, which radically enhances a person's overall cardiovascular health. Every Salat that we offer is similar to exercising daily, which improves the overall functioning of the organs in the body and regulates the secretion of glands and the circulation. A study revealed that waking up right before sunrise, just before production of the hormone melatonin stops, reduces the risk of heart attacks, which happen most commonly at that time. Waking up and performing yoga exercises, meditation, and prayers will act as good stewardship of the heart, and that's the wisdom behind praying specifically at that time of the day.

According to modern science, one of the healthiest forms of exercise is yoga. Yoga, like Salat, rejuvenates the overall bodily mechanisms. It not only aims to keep a person physically fit but also works toward improving their mental well-being. Salat is a substitute for stress and anxiety, which yoga combats too. Yoga therapy seeks to bring peace and harmony to a person by laying all aspects of their life, involving the physical, social, spiritual, and psychological, as well as creating a full circle of equanimity. This is precisely what Salat strives to do: to bring about absolute harmony and peace within an individual. You see, it was never about being punished or going to hell if you didn't pray to and worship God. It's not about who is right and who is wrong. It's about knowing the truth, doing your body, spirit, or health justice, thus gleaning the benefits of rejecting earlier harmful experiences. Not doing that can lead you astray, and who knows what's in store for us in the afterlife? Where will we go when we die?

Things turn out best for the people who make
the best of the way things turn out.

— John Wooden

＊　＊　＊

CHAPTER 5:
ANGELS AND DEMONS – ROAD
TO HEAVEN AND HELL

*Don't search for heaven and hell in the future. Both
are now present. Whenever we manage to love without
expectations, calculations, negotiations, we are indeed
in heaven. Whenever we fight, hate, we are in hell.*

— Shams Tibrizi

The Devil's Realm: Sins, Hatred, and Revolutions

We often question why evil exists and why God allows it to enter our lives. To understand, we have to go back to the source and root of its existence, the devil. What is the logic behind the devil, and how did we as humans come up with such an entity in the first place? Why have people always believed in angels and demons and instinctively followed or willfully resisted faith? Why do we have such a broad spectrum of ideas on the subject? Did we devise a fairy tale out of what our ancestors envisioned? Did it occur as a sequence and series of divinations due to deep meditative states? Did the universe guide us through its plants? Have historical personages influenced our beliefs because of encounters with paranormal presences? Let's take a closer look at the root cause of evil.

The Devil's Personality

Regardless of how we define the devil, all options will lead to the same conclusion: evil exists in many forms. The devil is not necessarily a scary red character with spiked horns and a hellish pitchfork. He could be dark or negative energy; he could be chaos, antimatter; or he could be something we cannot comprehend. The image of Satan that humans invented was an archetype so that we could grasp what evil is. It does not mean that it's an accurate depiction. Still, why does it exist? Why don't we live in a world free of evil, famine, hatred, fear, cruelty, and darkness? Why can't we all live in a happy place where everyone is treated fairly and equally with no trouble whatsoever? If God is so powerful and loves us, why isn't he granting His creation what we deserve? The answer exists and always has, but we choose to turn a blind eye or, even worse, try to muster facts to disprove His existence.

Myths have always been around to explain the creation and nature of our world. In a modern analogy, Marvel comics and movies conceived heroic characters and villains to illustrate great feats of bravery and cowardice. Our story began when Adam and Eve lived in paradise, and it was intended for all of God's creations to live in a tranquil place free of evil and darkness. Sin did not exist in any form; hence, Adam and Eve knew nothing of hate, division, envy, anger, agony, or fear. They had abundance and lived in bliss. Imagine if you were born into a world where everything was perfect! There is zero poverty; you are always healthy; there is no darkness, no illness, no wars, nothing evil that you know today, and you were utterly oblivious of these things. How would you come to appreciate the blessings that you have, then? How would you relish light if you didn't know darkness? How would you appreciate abundance if scarcity didn't exist? How would you enjoy being wealthy if there were no poverty—who would serve the rich if there were no poor? Savor good health if illnesses were absent? Or appreciate peace if there were no war? Cherish kindness if there were no envy, experience love if there were no hate? The only way you can appreciate something good is by intentionally allowing its polar opposite to exist. It had to exist in the first place and be witnessed across generations so it became an unwavering reminder of what we should treasure. Otherwise, we wouldn't be able to identify good things, and we would never appreciate what we have.

The idea of evil's permanence in our life is a preparation for the afterlife, or else we will never understand the tenacity of happiness. We go through suffering in different ways but ultimately our pain serves us all to the same end. It is indeed a delusion that some people are happier than others just because they're wealthier or healthier. Wealthy people sometimes never find genuine friendships or love, whereas healthy people may find honest love and friendships, yet financial struggles pose comparable pain in their lives. People choose to embrace their victimhood and take for granted that others have sounder lives, unaware of the struggles they go through. We take for granted what is abundant in our own lives, and we are blind to what is copious for us may be the root cause of others' grief. This is how Adam and Eve were oblivious to the blessings they possessed, and this is precisely why God created the devil, to introduce pain, divisions, and struggles (in different ways) into our lives so that we would come to recognize what we have and appreciate what He tried to bestow on us to begin with.

Everything in our lives revolves around the balance of good and evil, yin and yang, light and dark, rich and poor, healthy and ill, happy and sad, hope and despair, and so on. Then what follows? Heaven and hell? Is there life after death and eternal consciousness? Are heaven and hell a human construct to glorify what's to come next?

We are only limited by what the mind is capable of imagining. There is a world beyond our reach that confounds our understanding of the universe. So, let's not limit our beliefs to what was ordained to us and realize that all that we know is a fragment of boundless potentialities.

Back to the archetypical story of when God created the devil for all the scenarios discussed above. He introduced seven deadly sins that define the root cause of many evils. These include pride, lust, wrath, greed, gluttony, envy, and sloth. Try to identify the most prominent ones by choosing what you feel is driving your shadow self or taking you over in general.

The Seven Deadly Sins

We are all different, thus each of us will perceive sins differently, some as harder to get rid of than others. We might be agents of several overpowering sins and a few that we cannot relate to at all, while others might display equal portions of every sin. I would like you to take your time in reading the following, and then based on your understanding of the concepts, rank your sins as to what you believe are the most conspicuous versus the least conspicuous ones in your life. Being aware of *your* deadly sins may be a good start to consciously eliminating them.

Pride

It was pride that changed angels into devils: it is humility that makes men as angels.

— St. Augustine

Pride has been called the root sin from which all other sins arise. It was the first sin that shook Satan when God ordered him to kneel before Adam and resulted in him being sent out of heavens. There's a reason this is considered the deadliest of all sins, and philosophers tend to reserve a special place for pride. The others are all bad, but the main reason pride is the deadliest is because it's the beginning of all sins. It takes pride to disobey what's meant to be for our own good. It takes pride not to surrender and to believe we are the most superior person in the world. It takes pride to please ourselves at the expense of everyone else. There's a fine line between that kind of pride and the pride we take in our work or have for our school, university, family, or country. Pride is not just going to make it seem like it's a fine line, but it's going to stir a debate about whether it's a sin at all. Many confuse this sin with being confident, ambitious, or patriotic, not realizing that thinking highly of ourselves as an individual or as a collective group only leads to narcissism, ethnic divisions, wars, and identity conflicts toward the other. We must remember we are least proud when we are alone.

Lust

Sex is the consolation you have when you can't have love.

— Gabriel Garcia Marquez

Lust is a powerful force that creates an intense desire for someone's body, an object, money, power, or any agent used to soothe your emotions. This fire caused by desire is the main reason there's suffering to begin with. The elimination of desire can end all the pain from someone's life. However, that's easier said than done. The problem here is that lust is confused with passion, in the form of attachment toward anything to attain perfection, when in reality life is not perfect and never will be; hence, it will be the ultimate reaction to all imperfection and suffering. Lust is considered to be the desire for sexual pleasure, but sexual desire in itself is good, and it's considered part of God's plan for humanity and essential for the procreation of life. When sexual desire is separated from God's love, it becomes disoriented and self-pleasing: this is considered lust. It's a pleasure bought with agonies, a delight shaded with anxiety, a content spread with fear, and a sin completed with sorrow.

Wrath

Whatever is begun in anger ends in shame.

— Benjamin Franklin

Making a clear distinction between wrath and anger is imperative. Anger is an emotional response and not a freely chosen moral act.

For example, if we witness someone stealing or committing an act of violence, or a son slapping their parent, we may impulsively feel angry. How we act upon it and how we control this anger is the difference between righteousness and wanting to avenge the act. How we manage our temper is vital in figuring out why that person acted the way they did. We cannot correct wrong with wrong, and we cannot show hate or exert violence on someone and not expect a reaction if not an escalation. We are all human, and if we start to view (not justify) that person's actions from the wisdom of pity or knowing the circumstances that led that person to act the way they did, it'll be much easier controlling our emotions.

Greed

For greed all nature is too little.

— Lucius Annaeus Seneca

Greed is a sin of desire, and it's as much as man denounces eternal gains for the sake of temporary materialistic desires. It's the never-ending need for material wealth or gain, ignoring the spiritual realm and its returns. Gandhi once said, "Earth provides enough to satisfy every man's need, but not every man's greed." Unfortunately, many lose sight of how much they need, and their desire to build on what they have spreads like wildfire. The real problem here is when it comes to materialism, the desire for wanting it quickly dies out once we attain it, it's a continual, vicious loop, a fake and deluded pursuit of happiness. Many people don't realize that getting and desiring more is like an animal chasing its tail: it's not going to make us happier. It may make us more content for a while, but only temporarily, and then we'll find ourselves wanting to jump into our next quest. It's no different from the carrot-and-stick analogy. We need to focus more on the qualities of the journey unreservedly and expect no prizes along the way; expecting moral dessert isn't how we should live our life.

Gluttony

The gluttons dig their own graves with their teeth.

— James Howell

Gluttony is very similar to lust and greed; the difference is it's subtler, especially in terms of excess eating or drinking. The reason this is considered a sin is that those who overindulge are not only prone to diseases and bring nothing but harm to themselves, but they also withhold someone else's share. The selfish act of choosing to eat or drink more than someone who is without and is dying is considered a sin. So, it's not just about consuming immoderate amounts of food and drink, but the capacity to receive or withstand something for the purpose of selfishness. There's a crucial difference between greed and gluttony: greed is an insufficiency in generosity and a failure in consideration of others, due to the compulsion to have, whereas gluttony is a failure of self-control.

Envy

Jealousy is the tie that binds, and binds, and binds.

— Helen Rowland

Envy might be defined as an insatiable desire for something based on resenting someone else's possession of it. It's an extreme feeling of jealousy of and discontent about someone else's features, abilities, looks, status, rewards, relationships, health, wealth, possessions, and so on. The real problem with envy is that it can lead someone to go to great lengths, to the point of theft, subtle or indirect evil acts, and even murder, and to justify those actions.

Sloth

What is right is often forgotten by what is convenient.

— Bodie Thoene

Being lazy or intentionally not helping those in need, even though it would be possible to, is the deadly sin of sloth. Turning a blind eye to someone in need or choosing not to work or be diligent is one of the ways of falling short in good deeds. We should live our lives through hard work and service to others. It is the most difficult sin to acknowledge as evil since it doesn't involve doing anything. Mental and physical activity is a way to maintain our health, and all we need to neglect that is doing the opposite: nothing.

* * *

The Devil's Knight

Aleister Crowley was one of the wickedest people on Earth. He was a controversial occultist who founded a religion defiantly opposing every other religion and who lived life according to his own dictum *"Do what thou wilt" shall be the whole of the law.* Now, this phrase was purposely designed to free humans from any restraint or order constituted by religion. The whole point of surrendering our spirit is resisting temptations that can accidentally and perhaps innocently harm our physical body and alter our conscious and unconscious mind. However, Crowley had a different point of view. He valued the self and considered it a spiritual act to do whatever one thought their ego desired, even if it meant separation from a united front. Crowley's questionable interests combined the erotic and the esoteric. He published exotic poetry, including a volume of verse explained by one of his critics as "the most disgusting piece of erotica in the English language." To give you an insight of his style, here are some Crowley quotes: "Happiness lies within one's self, and the way to dig it out is cocaine." "I slept with faith and found a corpse in my arms on awakening; I drank and danced all night with doubt and found her a virgin in the morning." "Sex is, directly or indirectly, the most powerful weapon in the armory of the Magician; and precisely because there is no moral guide, it is indescribably dangerous. I have given a great many hints, especially in *Magick*, and *The Book of Thoth*—some of the cards are almost blatantly revealing; so, I have been rapped rather severely over the knuckles for giving children matches for playthings. My excuse has been that they have already got the matches, that my explanations have been directed to add conscious precautions to the existing automatic safeguards."

Crowley also became involved in secretive cults like the Hermetic Order of the Golden Dawn. Gradually he enhanced his own set of beliefs, which were based on Eastern, ancient Egyptian, and various other traditions. His sexual conceptions were equally various. He was never monogamous: he took many lovers, both male and female, and practiced a form of sex-magic. He stated that an ancient Egyptian spirit dictated the Law of Thelema to him. It laid out the critical fundamentals of life, as Crowley said "the pursuit of each individual's will, unconstrained by popular opinion, law, or traditional ethics." He moved to Sicily in 1920, where he founded the Abbey of Thelema as the headquarters for his new religion. There he sought spiritual enlightenment, declaring himself as an Ipssissimus— beyond the gods. He also experimented frequently with sex and drugs. An Englishman died in mysterious circumstances during one of Crowley's rituals, in which the man was said to have drunk the blood of a cat. The Italian fascist government and the British press were equally appalled. Crowley was deported from Italy, the abbey shut down, and the group dissolved. Although appalled, downtrodden, and addicted to heroin, Crowley never lacked followers. He designed a new sequence of tarot cards and commentated on it at some length in his *Book of Thoth* in 1944. Crowley died in Hastings, in 1947.

Only twelve people attended Crowley's funeral; he wasn't keen on spreading good words or reputation and could care less about the love of people. Although he was not a delightful figure, his impact on people was much more significant after his death. His religion inspired many to conspire against God and religions in general. Through the media, many of his top-tier followers encouraged sex and drug revolution. Society is deteriorating, and these are gradually becoming acceptable... *Do what thou wilt.* We are only considered civilized if we accept others' individuality, but what contradicts that is when we voice our opinion regarding any matter that opposes individuality, we are criticized and frowned upon. How is this freedom of speech, then? If you trump someone's right to voice their opinion (no matter what it is), isn't that against exercising freedom of speech?

Believers in this day and age are stomped on, and when they speak up, they are shut down: it's considered discourteous. When nonbelievers speak up, it is tolerable because it's okay to oppose the notion of a creator, to criticize and offend religion. In what civilized world is reverence conditional and one-sided? Cultures and beliefs are slandered for being traditional, and they're alleged to be uncivilized, yet freedom of speech is upheld in the very same societies that are judging. What a time to be alive!

* * *

CERN: Discovering the "God Particle"

One of the largest experiments in the world devoted to research in the physics of matter at an infinitely small scale... You are invited to tumble down the rabbit hole into the wonderland of ALICE. CERN.

The global elite is now in the process of revealing what they have been hiding for many years. There is a spiritual war on our planet at this very moment. Part of the Gotthard Base Tunnel opening ceremony in Switzerland on June 1, 2016, portrayed an occult-riddled ritual that featured Baphomet copulating with a human woman, the bride of Satan giving birth, all bluntly showcased along with an untold number of Satanic connotations. Meanwhile, in front of CERN's headquarters at the Large Hadron Collider, we see a contemptuous statue of Shiva the god of destruction. Moreover, the CERN movie *Symmetry* makes their intentions clear: they are actively trying to break the barrier between what is seen and unseen. The elite also seems hell-bent on ushering in their New World Order

Beast System, and at this point, they have stopped hiding it. Would it surprise any of you to find out Darwin's theory in his book *The Origins of Species* is also nothing more than lies based on false science to get the world's population to dismiss the notion of one true creator altogether? If the elite could get most of the world to believe this beautiful globe and all who inhabit it were nothing more than a random fluke, if not an infectious virus, it could get humanity to disarm its spiritual shields, therefore making it far easier to direct the global system they sought, coated by the one they secretly solicit, Satan. Spiritual warfare on this planet is alive and well—and you have been lied to.

I am gradually linking everything that had happened from Adam's descent to the Final Deception. It's all inevitably building up in that direction, from both sides—good and bad. There's plenty of motive, and awareness has reached an all-time high now, with globalization exposing people to all sorts of information. How close are we to Judgment Day? Let's look at what we know, as far as usable information is concerned.

Stephen Hawking, a very well-known scientist, didn't believe in God's existence until the CERN project came to light. To break down the project into simple terms, there's a collider tube extending from Switzerland to France, and it's used to collide the smallest of smallest quantum particles together to get to what they're looking for: antimatter. They're looking for the building blocks of life that glued everything into existence, in its initial unbonded form after the occurrence of the big bang.

Mapping the secrets of the universe: ATLAS is a particle physics experiment at the Large Hadron Collider (LHC) at CERN that is searching for discoveries in

the head-on collisions of protons of extraordinarily
high energy. ATLAS will learn about the basic forces
that have shaped our Universe since the beginning
of time, and that will determine its fate. Among the
possible unknowns are extra dimensions of space.

— CERN

* * *

Let's put things into perspective: the atomic bomb used on Hiroshima was made out of a few grams of matter. Matter is anything that is seen and touched. Antimatter or dark matter is whatever is left in the void of space. Now there is no such thing as absolute void simply because the fabric of space is made of something invisible holding our planets and stars in a netlike manner (gravitational force), keeping them in balance; otherwise, stars and planets would've kept falling endlessly and with no specific purpose. That invisible force is what they're trying to discover, the opposite of matter. Now, it sounds insane to be looking for something made out of nothing; it doesn't make any sense, but they know it's out there. The experiments already conducted have unveiled interestingly speculative findings. A few grams of antimatter are so unstable: their destructive power is equivalent to four Hiroshima bombs and cannot be easily confined. It's being contained at CERN, and they're creating more and more of it. It is energy in a negative form that brings equilibrium to this world; hence, the presence of matter. Without antimatter, matter won't exist and vice versa. If the antimatter is the chaotic and unstable state of matter, then it can only mean that more negative energy will attract more of that same energy, more of what goes against the order of matter, thus creating an imbalance of energy. Now, here is a spine-chilling conclusion: negative energy draws more negative energy, and they know very well that even a few grams of antimatter created can destroy this planet and consequently attract the strongest adverse reactions in existence.

"Out of this door might come something, or we might send something through it." Dr. Sergio Bertolucci, Director for Research and Scientific Computing at CERN later confirmed that indeed, there would be an open door, but that even with the power of the LHC at his disposal, he would only be able to hold it open "a very tiny lapse of time, ten to twenty-six seconds… [but] during that infinitesimal amount of time we would be able to peer into this open door, either by getting something out of it or sending something into it."

* * *

Many experiments were conducted in CERN's underground labs, with numerous incidents of people encountering paranormal activities and frequent nightmares reported, some purportedly even being possessed by unknown entities. In other words, the creation of antimatter from a mystical standpoint is a portal to the spiritual world—the unseen dimension. Most of the research is still theoretical, so even though findings are still unexplored, the intention of the project is quite clear. We are blindly and intentionally headed toward uncharted territory. What has been publicly disclosed is that scientists at CERN are trying to discover the God particle; this is partially true, but not entirely. The great deception may not be in the literal sense of people going into an apocalyptic war. It's exhibited in terms of disordered exploitations of turmoil, hence more chaos, more negativity, more wars, more conflicts, more division, more hatred, more famine, and so on.

Concept of Time and Black Holes

And he shall speak great words against the most High,
and shall wear out the saints of the most High, and think
to change times and laws: and they shall be given into his
hand until a time and times and the dividing of time.

— Bible, CH7: V25.

Think of time as a parade, and imagine that you're standing in the middle of the parade observing only what is happening in front of you. From where you stand, you can't see what happened at the beginning of the parade, and you don't know what will happen at the end. However, if you're in a helicopter above, you can observe all that is happening in the parade from start to finish. This analogously demonstrates how what is called the hidden dimension works with time. There is no time in this dimension. Spiritual beings can zoom in at any point in time and access the past, present, or future and even transit between them. The human construct of a time line was necessary because we observe time from a present standpoint, where we only have access to one dimension. The idea of not seeing or interacting with those spiritual beings is beyond our comprehension. There's a reason we can only hear a limited range of sound frequencies, and then beyond the margins we are deaf to higher or lower measurements. Whales, for instance, have a wider marginal aural spectrum. The same applies to our sense of sight: we can only see what's between infrared and ultraviolet rays, but beyond both margins is undetected. Accordingly, when it comes to space-time and dimensions, our mind is bound by limitations. We are restricted to what we perceive based on the perspicacity of our sensory neurons.

For all we know, what is yet to happen has already happened in the realm of God.

> *For if God spared not the angels that sinned, but cast them down to hell, and delivered them into chains of darkness, to be reserved unto judgment.*

— Bible, CH2: V4.

> *And they had a king over them, which is the angel of the bottomless pit, whose name in the Hebrew tongue is Abaddon, but in the Greek tongue hath his name Apollyon.*

— Bible, CH9: V11.

The revelation above may infer black holes for various reasons. A black hole is a fallen star with gravity so strong that nothing can escape from it, including light. It's also so dense that it bends the fabrics of the universe so low to the point of singularity. This means that anything around its gravitational vicinity, whether it's a planet, star, or asteroid, will be crushed into a singular point. Time also dilates and becomes slow around a black hole, and it becomes even slower the closer you get to the bottom. The whole construct of time collapses at the bottom point. It has been described in the Bible that fallen angels and Lucifer are trapped in something similar to what we know as a black hole.

The European Organization for Nuclear Research at CERN, physicists, and engineers are digging for the fundamental structure of the universe. They use the planet's largest, most complex, and most sophisticated scientific instruments to study the primary constituents of matter—the fundamental atoms. The atoms are made to collide together at almost the speed of light. The process gives the physicists clues about how the particles interact and provide insights into the fundamental laws of nature.

"We have calculated the energy at which we expect to detect these mini black holes in gravity's rainbow [a new theory]. If we do detect mini black holes at this energy, then we will know that both gravity's rainbow and extra dimensions are correct," Dr. Mir Faizal told phys.org. "Just as many parallel sheets of paper, which are two dimensional objects [breadth and length] can exist in a third dimension [height], parallel universes can also exist in higher dimensions.... We predict that gravity can leak into extra dimensions, and if it does, these miniature black holes can be produced at the LHC... parallel universes. What we mean is real universes in extra dimensions." - The Telegraph, March 2015.

* * *

The monument to Shiva, the god of destruction, outside the CERN facility, depicts the gateway to the hidden dimension through a gravitational force similar to a black hole. *Angels and Demons*, a movie based on Dan Brown's book, had a portion filmed at CERN's Large Hadron Collider. Several interesting theories were discussed in this movie that I found quite appealing. A large part of CERN is located in the territory of Saint-Genis-Pouilly. The town and a temple were dedicated to Apollyon, the destroyer (Shiva/Horus).

All the magnets on the LHC are electromagnets.
The main dipoles generate powerful 8.4 Tesla
magnetic fields—more than 100,000 times more
powerful than the Earth's magnetic field.

— CERN

The whole analogy of the black hole is derived from the ancient story that suggests that God will allow Satan life till Judgment Day. If the black hole collapses, the constructs of time will too; then it only makes sense to dilate, stop, or loop time to avoid judgment. CERN has addressed this specific theory through the ouroboros they keep displaying in their advertisements, and their obsession with time is reflected in different ways.

> *And in those days shall men seek death, and shall not find*
> *it; and shall desire to die, and death shall flee from them.*
>
> — Bible, CH9: V6.

* * *

Ouroboros is a symbol of a serpent in an infinite motion of biting, devouring, or eating its own tail. It reflects the cyclic nature of the universe: creation out of destruction, life out of death. The serpent eats its tail to sustain its life in an eternal cycle of renewal. Therefore, the whole concept of ouroboros, Shiva the god of destruction, and the dangers that come with the CERN project of studying and collecting antimatter is not for the purpose of annihilation, but it's to recreate life as we know it. If we can understand how life was formed, how the big bang occurred and brought life into existence, then there is no reason to be afraid of destroying what we already know for the intention of recreation. We are playing God in this game and challenging no one but ourselves.

> *...For our light affliction, which is but for a moment, worketh*
> *for us a far more exceeding and eternal weight of glory;*
> *while we look not at the things which are seen, but at the*

things which are not seen: for the things which are seen are
temporal; but the things which are not seen are eternal.

— Bible, CH4: V17–18.

* * *

A black hole is the zone of space that has an immense gravitational field where no matter, rays, or even light can escape it. Before
2011, astrophysicists were not able to accurately report the stars falling into black holes portent, but not anymore. The total occurrences
of stars collapsing into black holes reported between then and 2016
have been three. There is an entire section in the Quran named "The
Star," and the first verse of that section is "By the Star. When it falls"
Quran, CH53: V1. The Quran then goes on to explain the features
of a place very similar to the description of the black hole. This place
in space is described, in verse 16 of chapter 53, as *very dark*. It's
explained as darkness covered or wrapped in darkness, which is not
surprising; space is a dark place after all. Even then, some areas are
darker than others, but nothing is more perplexing than a black hole.
Black holes have such an immense force of gravity: nothing, not even
light can escape from them, which are why they are black.

As a consequence, they are masked from direct observation.
In spite of that, they unveil themselves indirectly, as scientists have
exceptional instruments that can support them in observing how
stars that are close to black holes behave in comparison to stars that
are not so close, due to the tremendous force of gravity that black
holes exert. Also, this helps them identify the location of black holes.

According to the Quran, when regular people stare right into
this dark field in space, they can't detect it accurately as their eyes

circumvent or bypass the boundary of this black sphere. They can only see beyond it or around it. It's as if this field behaves like a barrel distortion or convex lens. The scientific term for this phenomenon is a *gravitational lens*. Light typically travels in straight uncurving beams, but approaching a black hole, the powerful gravitational force curves and warps light rays around it, forming a visible dent on the surrounding matter. Astrophysicists have confirmed that a black hole bends light to make it function as a cosmic magnifying glass, granting astronomers a stretched view of an even more distant space behind it. However, the Quran proclaims an intriguing suggestion concerning this matter. In verse 17 of chapter 53, it states, "The eyesight [of the Prophet Muhammad] did not swerve, nor did it pass beyond the boundary. He certainly saw it as one of the greatest signs of his Lord." Could this verse point to the notion that the Prophet Muhammad had access to the gravitational field of a black hole and on to some other dimension? Alternatively, did he see it as something else we still are unaware of?

Moreover, the Quran defines this field's shape broad at the top with sloping sides into a tight tunnel at the bottom, almost shaped like a funnel. In verse 14 of chapter 53, it mentions, "By the finite jujube tree." It is paralleled to the shape of a jujube tree, which matches the corresponding description to the one I just described. A black hole makes a very deep dip in space-time, and that is why it seems to resemble a funnel.

With that verse, "By the finite jujube tree," the Quran declares that this field is finite. So how does this claim stack up against the science? Not long ago, it was speculated that black holes had infinite gravitational-field strength, and a journey into a black hole would be a one-way trip. Once you traversed the point of the horizon at which light can't escape, there'd be no going back. Researchers such as Jorge Pullin, Rodolfo Gambini, and Gerard Hooft have latterly proved the opposite; they confirm that energy can indeed escape black holes and that black holes are finite. This means that black holes don't collapse infinitely but rather drop to the point of singularity or function as a portal to another universe or dimension. The esteemed British physicist Stephen Hawking supported this case and further suggested that there could be a way out of a black hole when he quipped, "If you feel you are in a black hole, don't give up. There's a way out. It might have a passage to another universe. But you couldn't come back to our Universe. So, although I am keen on space flight, I am not going to try that."

The Quran testifies by the falling star that the Prophet Muhammad reached a field, which is one of God's greatest signs. The details and steps of such an occurrence are unknown; all we know is that the gravitational field is much darker than its surroundings and no one can see this area directly as his or her eyesight will swerve and pass beyond its boundary. We have now heard that this field is finite and/or a portal to another dimension. So, it would seem that the Quran and astrophysicists agree on that end. What happens next? And will we ever create a similar gravitational force that is colossal enough to warp our dimension into another? I guess the future holds that answer.

* * *

Many consider conspiracy theories farfetched and Illuminati and Freemasonry agendas to be nothing but exaggerated paranoia for those who fear being controlled. In that case, what are their aspirations, and what do they seek? First things first: we should be cognizant that the Illuminati is an anonymous group of people who seek a new world order by controlling the masses. They successfully managed to control the world's economy by fabricating the modern monetary system. What's behind their agenda? Also, what kind of higher order do they want the masses to follow? Is it a divine order? I think not. Then who are they? Before jumping to conclusions, let's look more closely at their instruments. The Illuminati is the same group of people who help fund the CERN project and use media as their prime means to brainwash people with their ideologies, and this, of course, happens subliminally—on a subconscious level.

Before being cynical about this, consider for a moment why the Emmy Awards in 2015 would have explicitly displayed CERN's logo? As you may have discerned, movies, songs, and video clips have been ethically deteriorating over time. This has happened ever so subtly to the point where the majority of the population is slowly normalizing everything promoted. This is taking place only because people are constantly bombarded with ideas, thoughts, and images that eventually numb their initial perception of it. Also, those who resist or revolt will soon become the outcast minority, which is a brilliant and effective maneuvering tactic in my opinion.

One dubious Hollywood sign of this is the famous Oscar award, which depicts a fallen angel! The face of light depicts the face of Lucifer, and of course, the best actors and actresses who portray their teachings and ideologies regularly get awarded! This is not even recognized as a fanciful conspiracy anymore as actors are explicitly showing gratitude to Satan on live TV. Christian Bale in his Golden Globes 2019 speech said, "Thank you, Satan, for giving me inspiration for playing this role" when he referred to his character, Dick Cheney, in a political satire.

BEYOND THE PRISON OF BELIEFS

Now, all of these theories may seem absurd, but if true, they pose mind-blowing possibilities. Whether those funding and working at CERN know what they're doing and the implications of what might happen is not even the real issue. It's the intention of their pursuits that's concerning.

On September 7, 2014, Stephen Hawking warned in an article in the Daily Mail, that following his predictions, our planet is unstable and, as a result, might collapse. Dr. Joseph Lykken, a respected theoretical physicist at the University of Chicago, supported Dr. Hawking's findings when he stated, "If you use all the physics that we know now and you do what you think is a straightforward calculation, it is bad news, and it may be that the universe we live in is inherently unstable. We're right on the edge where the universe can last for a long time, but eventually, it should go 'boom.' There's no principle that we know of that would put us right on edge." Dr. Benjamin Allanach, another reputable theoretical physicist, at the University of Cambridge, further promoted the reason for this instability when he talked about a specific particle that subsists in the universe called the Higgs boson particle. "The observed 126, Higgs boson mass, seems to imply the universe does not exist in the lowest possible energy state but is in fact positioned in a slightly unusual place. If the Higgs mass were really 127 GeV and the top mass was a little lower than its most likely value, then actually the universe would be completely stable, and the vacuum would be in the true minimum."

Under the most basic suppositions, the calculated mass of Higgs could indicate that the universe is unstable and predestined to fall apart. So, according to various physicists' careful forecasts and calculations, we're virtually all condemned! The Quran verifies the predictions of physicists such as Hawking, Lykken, and Allanach: the possibility of a collapsing universe is real. Nevertheless, the Quran then goes on to reassure us that God prevents the universe from collapsing when He addresses it thus: "God holds the heaven from falling on earth." Quran, CH22: V65. Besides, God prohibits the wipeout of the universe by affirming, "God holds the heavens and the earth lest they are wiped out." Quran, CH35: V41. So, what may an apocalypse or end of the world be like, exactly? Also, what do the Higgs boson particles have to do with all this? The British physicist Peter Higgs, in 1960, theorized the existence of minuscule particles that we cannot detect even under the most powerful, cutting-edge microscopes. These particles are responsible for giving objects mass and are actually in us and all around us. Without Higgs boson, everything we perceive around us, including you and me, would have no mass and accordingly cease to exist.

Many physicists at that time agreed with Dr. Higgs regarding the existence of this particle, as he presented solid proof to confirm his theory. They named these subatomic particles after him and called them Higgs particles. On March 14, 2013, scientists at CERN tentatively verified the existence of the Higgs boson particle. To fully confirm the discovery of it, CERN produced the infamous Large Hadron Collider at the cost of approximately ten billion dollars to imitate the conditions of the creation of the universe or the big bang.

In 1993, a group of British physicists urged the science minister at the time, William Waldegrave, to contribute in the construction of the Large Hadron Collider to help prove the existence of the Higgs particle. The minister had no idea what they were talking about, so he proposed an award of a vintage bottle of champagne to the scientist who came up with the simplest explanation of the Higgs field and the Higgs boson. Professor David Miller earned the prize with his distinct analogy. "Imagine a cocktail party of political party workers who are uniformly distributed across the floor, all talking to their nearest neighbors. If the ex-Prime Minister, Margaret Thatcher, enters the room many workers will run toward her and form a cluster around her. As she moves, other workers run toward her, while the ones she has left return to their places. Because of the knot of people running toward her forming a cluster and then returning back to their spots, she acquires mass. These clusters, which run toward Ms. Thatcher and then disappear as they return back to their spots are analogous to Higgs bosons."

If that's the Higgs field, what is the Higgs boson, then? Let's imagine our group of people is spread evenly across the hall. "Now consider a rumor passing through our room full of people. Those near the door run to hear it first and cluster together to get the details, then they return to their original spots and tell their neighbors, who then run and cluster together to hear it too. Then they return to their original spots and tell their next neighbors and so on. The result will be a wave of clusters running across the room that disappear as soon as they run. These clusters are analogous to Higgs bosons."

To conclude, Higgs boson is an evasive subatomic particle that can't be seen but gives particles mass or matter. It is what gives shape, size, and mass to everything in existence. The problem with the Higgs particle that the LHC has discovered is that it holds a mass of about 126 GeV (giga-electron volts) and this made physicists anxious, as they understand it should be 127 GeV. Physicists such as Stephen Hawking, Joseph Lykken, and Benjamin Allanach considered this discrepancy might very well mean the collapse of the universe, as everything will become massless. The Quran also assures that, when the world ends, "It is the day when people will be like scattered moths, and the mountains shall be as loosened wool" Quran, CH101: V4–5. People like moths and mountains like wool analogize mass loss.

The legendary Marvel movie *Avengers: Infinity War* visually depicts this complex phenomenon when Thanos turns everyone into massless cosmic dust. Before the massacre, he has to collect six infinity stones that represent reality. *Thanos* is an acronym for the locations of the infinity stones, where each letter is the beginning letter of the infinity-stone casings: Tesseract (Space Gem), Heimdall (Soul Gem), Aether (Reality Gem), Necklace (Time Gem), Orb (Power Gem), and Scepter (Mind Gem). Turning all of this into cosmic dust is more horrifying than asteroids pelting the Earth's surface.

In chapter 81 of the Quran, there's a section where God outlines the event details of the end of the world. Two specific verses that are of surpassing importance to us are: "So verily, I God, swear by clusters you can't see, as soon as they run, they disappear." In these verses (15 and 16), the words used in formal Arabic are more nuanced, and translations don't capture the full meaning. Three words in particular are used: *Khonas* and *Al Jawary Al Konas*. *Khonas* denotes something invisible, *Al Jawary* refers to something that is running, and *Al Konas* means something that disappears and returns to its original position. So, if we combine these three words, we are addressing invisible clusters that run and then disappear virtually as soon as they appear. As soon as they start running, they stop and disappear. So, what are these quantum clusters that the Quran is defining? They are none other than the elusive Higgs bosons particles, which delineates why the end of the universe may come about not because of volcanic activity, groundbreaking earthquakes, hurricanes, tornadoes, storms, meteor showers, or an asteroid hitting the Earth—the universe will end due to mass loss.

* * *

The Angel's Realm: Patience, Love and Peace

Each life is made up of mistakes and learning, waiting
and growing, practicing patience and being persistent.

— Billy Graham

When your mind is all over the place, you become so consumed it eventually shuts off and wears out. That's when your heart will take over, your feelings will bring you closer to the truth, and you will flourish. You'll discover who you are through emotions, not thoughts. Words cannot explain anything that is real. The best philosophers and hopeless romantics in the world haven't been able to come up with the perfect description of love. Throughout centuries of romance and poetry, not one person has been able to spell out the magic of love or adequately convey its extremity. "You have to keep breaking your heart until it opens," Rumi said. The same goes for consciousness, spirit, and God. No one can make intelligible the parameters or linguistically contain such matters. My instinctive theory suggests that whatever is real is inexplicable. Whatever is corporeal or palpable and can be effortlessly expounded is an illusion. In other words, anything real depicts the intangible reality including but not limited to love, spirit, and belief in oneself and God. These things are difficult to explain: it's hard to come close to their true essence using words of eloquence. Anything tangible, on the other hand, is life as we perceive it, something of material form, whether it's our body, money, objects, or assets that can be described with ease; these are nothing but a deception of reality.

Love and patience are essential. You need love (pure love, not just attraction), and it doesn't matter how long you've been attached to a particular situation that you won't let go of. Love itself is therapeutic; patience is also crucial, as important as love. Patience helps you grow in many ways as a person. It takes a lot of discipline and self-control, and the more patient you are the wiser you become.

> *Patience is not sitting and waiting; it is foreseeing. It is looking at the thorn and seeing the rose, looking at the night and seeing the day. Lovers are patient and know that the moon needs time to become full.*

> — Rumi.

* * *

Love is patient. However, acquiring patience is one of the most challenging responsibilities to overcome. I recognized that patience is a direct rejoinder of love. If you love someone, you are going to make sure you do your best to be patient with that person, and frankly, it is as straightforward as it sounds. If you love someone, you let them open up and speak their mind when you want to hear it the least. "Patience is not simply the ability to wait—it's how we behave while we're waiting," says Joyce Meyer. Love requires a conscious effort to put yourself in someone else's shoes. It demands a conscious effort to anticipate a positive outcome in any circumstance. At any given moment, we have to remind ourselves repeatedly how important it is to stand for inner peace, how much you love this person, and how much you love yourself. The most potent gift you possess is your mind. Your mind has the power to do everything; it has the potential to love, to be patient, and to be happy. Ralph Waldo Emerson said, "Adopt the pace of nature: her secret is patience."

Naturally, we are very eager to get what we want immediately, disregarding everything but our thoughts and ourselves. Only our difficulties are significant to us, and the notion that others experience hardships in life too is overlooked because we are often preoccupied with our conditions. Listening grants you the moment to understand a person fully and genuinely. When you listen, you acquire something you never predicted, but when you speak, you are repeating what you already know. Envision arguing with a loved one: it drags on and remains unresolved because someone denied refraining from speaking and listening to the other's pain. Imagine if you both refrain from your desires: the place would be overcome with love and grief at the same time, but all that would be left is love. It would be love that compels you to listen to what they are feeling rather than solely focusing on your pain.

Patience and diligence, like faith, remove mountains.

— William Penn

* * *

Many believe that time is money and that there's no time to be patient or to love. The truth is if you love someone, patience for that person and yourself is wealth. We have to accept the moments where demonstrating patience may be the most significant promise for an impediment to be resolved. Patience requires a resilient effort to execute but is most gratifying when achieved. You have to remind yourself in the moment to be patient and to manifest love both for the other and yourself. The first person you need to be patient with is yourself. It opens you to a deeper understanding of yourself and the world. We have to set ourselves free from life's drama and seeing ourselves as victims. There's an extraordinary power in not taking things personally. Everyone wants to be loved and fears not being loved. Underneath that fear is the love that never ceases. Sink into that love and everything changes. Love and patience in many situations command pure selflessness, realizing that is the core of love. It is precisely what everyone should strive for, not only with loved ones, family, friends, or God, but preferably those people that serve you in cafes, clean your house or office, or make you coffee—that is where you need to be selfless the most. Lately, I have practiced altruism much more than usual, and I have realized how true is the proverb *You reap what you sow.* We undervalue the power of love and patience as a healing source. Love is a delightful encounter that is either taken advantage of or not fully appreciated. In every relationship—whether between lovers, family, or friends—if love is not the essence, it will fall apart. If love is in the core of that relationship, the opposite will take place.

Every great dream begins with a dreamer. Always remember,
you have within you the strength, the patience, and the
passion to reach for the stars to change the world.

— Harriet Tubman

*   *   *

When you're disconcerted or frustrated with someone, remember the power of love and how much you can achieve to overcome any hardship. Whoever believed that *Patience is a virtue* was perhaps waiting for the best things in life to happen to them. Most relationships in this day and age need the overpowering ubiquity of patience. We don't spend our lives expelling obstacles and going through them, we don't compromise easily on things, and we unquestionably look for the easy way out when we're running out of patience to face the slightest misunderstanding or conflict in a relationship. We have become less forgiving. We judge others and circumstances more viciously and make snap decisions. We display indifference when we should bestow kindness, and we never have the time to deal with arrogance, so we decide to quit or sweep matters under the carpet. All this provokes impatience and changes the heart of our being and, ultimately, impacts our relationships.

Patience and perseverance have a magical effect before
which difficulties disappear, and obstacles vanish.

— John Quincy Adams

* * *

A heavenly virtue that we need to master is the art of holding on to something or someone you unconditionally love until the end. No matter how bad things may seem or how far circumstances have gone, never leave. Never display apathy, and never run out of patience. Absorb and let everything go, and your willpower will never abandon you. Upholding the true covenant of tolerance, in tough times, is the definitive doorway to heaven.

I am certainly not going to lecture on how you should learn to be more patient, but I will surely insist on how it makes the dynamic between two people more worthwhile. No one is whole, and the idea of perfection is unsound, so you can view it as subjectively as you want. It's okay to slip and learn from your mistakes and move on. This teaches us ample patience. Also, with patience comes more space to feel everything without the denials getting under your skin and making you jump into false conclusions. There are various ways one may lose patience with their partner. At the start of any relationship, patience is vital. One person will always be ahead of the other on the love graph. One might still be staggering or unsure while the other is already anxiously anticipating beginning their life together. If you're the one waiting, wait with hope, promise, and positivity. Let the other person obtain more perspective and grow to where you are. Impatience can show you that you have not examined your thoughts or feelings enough before diving into a relationship. Give yourself and the other a dose of patience. Love will flourish and eventually conquer if you do. Consider this quote, widely attributed to Julius Caesar: "It is easier to find men who will volunteer to die than to find those who are willing to endure pain with patience."

Getting regular reminders from your past and acting on them in your present is expected. What you can do, however, is try giving up the excess baggage that you have stored and healing yourself first. Communicating with your partner about past anxieties should be reasonable and healthy. It helps you recover, and this healing will inescapably bring you patience to face the present by being more forgiving in your relationship. Patience in a relationship persists the test of endurance. It is not about disregarding the other person's imperfections and absurdities and sweeping them under the carpet.

Patience teaches us to interact healthily regarding the differences you notice in their habits, the incompatibilities, or even the pernicious attitudes and to discuss them. It only encourages two people to open up and trust each other more. If the other recognizes that you patiently understand something you don't approve about them, they will begin to meet you halfway. It's a gradual process, but you have to follow through. The aspiration is not to change them but to discuss your concerns in a patient and salutary manner. *The test of good manners is to be patient with the bad ones.* Solomon Ibn Gabirol

When you face a challenging person or circumstance, your involuntary reaction may be to protect yourself. When this occurs, it usually pulls you into drama and away from your center. In developing patience, you give yourself space and time to find the calm waters of wisdom as well as compassion and to see the bigger picture of what is going on beyond the initial outbursts. It is vital to speak up about wrongdoings or injustice, but make sure that your claims stem from a position of wholeness, not from resistance or ego. That will only lead to greater grief for everyone. Acting with vengeance or imprudently will only fuel the flame of anger or hate. Our fight-or-flight response is a primal instinct that kept us safe in the jungle. However, we no longer live in the wilderness. Patience gives you extra breathing space around your racing mind. It offers an augmented view, even in narrow perspectives. It is not easily fostered and often grows through adversity and misfortunes. It is like a gentle, aromatic flower that can thrive within the drought of a desert.

Struggles often serve to release the wisdom, patience, and strength we all possess but too seldom demonstrate.

— Jim Stovall

* * *

When you feel like life is a charging bull aimed straight at your heart and all you face are difficulties, hindrances, and barriers, you may be summoned to soften, surrender, and foster patience. Patience keeps your soul warm and open, while your mind remains composed and still. With inner balance, you can avail yourself of the current moment more thoroughly. Patience is deceptively compelling and transformative. It opens you to a more profound perception of yourself and the world and helps you reconnect with the love that has always resided within you.

The best lesson I ever learned about love was to be patient. I've been through the pains and ordeals that love can cast. I've also experienced an exquisite and special kind of love. Throughout my experiences, I have learned many lessons and grown considerably. I never knew what it truly meant to be patient about love…or maybe I never listened. When we are young, it seems like we can't wait to find it, so much so that it looks like we can sometimes forget or not even realize what it means to be in love unconditionally.

> *Patience is waiting, not passively waiting. That*
> *is laziness. But to keep going when the going*
> *is hard and slow—that is patience.*
>
> — Leo Tolstoy.

If you feel you have come only so far on your spiritual journey, be certain there is a more balanced approach to life. You want to be free from pain, yet here you are again, frustrated in the realm of affliction. Too often, when we face difficulty, we add fuel to the fire by criticizing ourselves for situations over which we had no control. Not only have we been criticized by others, but we may criticize ourselves as well with thoughts such as: *How could I have reacted instead? How did I end up in this position? When will I transcend these irrational emotions and live with elevated steadiness?*

Patience is the companion of wisdom.

— St. Augustine

* * *

It's painful to be judged or to bear the negative moods of others. However, it's equally painful to judge yourself in return. If you love yourself and rest in a position of wholeness, the highs and downfalls of others' states and the ever-changing nature of each transient day will pass over you like varying weather. However, if you are attached to what others think about you and are expecting their approval or praise, criticism hurts twice as much.

Trees that are slow to grow bear the best fruit.

— Molière

* * *

Practice humility and patience for your indiscretion. It is easy to point fingers—we all have dangerous tendencies. You know you can hurt someone and might naturally spill negativity right back at someone who points it in your direction. We are very likely to treat others the way we treat ourselves. When you are patient for your own sake, the way you misjudge, inflict pain, and own others causes you to evolve. You develop dignified patience and understanding of the same tendencies in others.

Patience teaches us to turn provocations into invocations,
to transform frustrations into celebrations.

— William Arthur Ward

* * *

We tend to take people's poor moods, emotional responses, criticism, and assaults personally. Of course, toxic energy aimed at you can hurt, yet, it doesn't have to. There is enormous power in not taking matters personally. When you do so, you strip away the mask and unveil more profound truths. You come to realize that everyone is troubled; everyone needs love and feels genuinely afraid they won't receive the love they require. Everyone will do the best they can when the opportunity presents itself.

Hurtful exchanges and cruel remarks can come so swiftly that you can barely identify what has gone wrong. When you exercise patience and take a step back from an unstable situation to breathe, you can control your impulsive reactions and examine the ingenious pathway of your spur-of-the-moment reactions. You can shift your consciousness inward and ask yourself: *What buttons did this person push? How did I feel? Why did I react the way I did? Why was I hurt? Is there something I am not seeing?*

He that can have patience can have what he will.

— Benjamin Franklin

*   *   *

Most people are just trying to get through their day. They may be bearing a heap of mental smoke, surging unhappiness, and unresolved hopes. When we are thoughtless, we act egotistically and narcissistically. Consumed with our needs and desires, we don't take notice of our external environment and the wants of others. Being sensitive to the external world beyond our ego is a skill nurtured through spiritual awakening. This is why we are here.

Every tragedy has a hero and a villain to keep the story going. To be free of life's melodramas, let go of perceiving yourself as the hero or a victim and others as antagonists. When you next meet an obvious adversary, please take a moment to reflect in order to steer clear of making their misery yours. Catherine Pulsifer said, "Learning patience can be a difficult experience, but once conquered you will find life is easier." Patience is the remedy for weakness, and impatience is the wreckage of strength. This quotation of Henry Wadsworth Longfellow wraps up human connections so elegantly: "If we could read the secret history of our enemies, we should find in each man's life sorrow and suffering enough to disarm all hostility." If we learn how to be patient, then we'll also be able to love unconditionally. Patience leads to love.

Everyone, including you, carries past wounds: deep childhood pains that lay peering until we accidentally pour our salty tears out. We mean no wrong. We collide into each other like diamonds, burnished by life unfolding. It is salubrious to try to see the best in others. When we do, we quit making them the cause of our misery. Instead, we begin adopting the efficacious opportunity each minute brings to take charge of and control our own lives. Observe that each person is acting to the best of their abilities at any given time. When we avoid taking matters personally and rest in love, our hearts will bloom into an overflowing river of compassion, and we will no longer feel hurt by our ignorance of others or feel the need to hurt anymore.

Rivers know this: there is no hurry.
We shall get there someday.

— *A. A. Milne*

* * *

Everyone fears that they won't be loved. Apply that thought to a person who pushes your buttons. Think of him or her in that way—just wanting love and fearing they will not get it. Then think of how you want to feel loved as well. Maybe we are not that different. Think of your parents this way, just desiring love, fearing they will not be loved back. Try to embody the fear they have, and realize you feel the same as well. Possibly, you are not that different. The love you desire is also the love they seek. The fear you get that you won't find love is the very same fear they encounter.

Imagine your friends and family members, and consider the way they yearn for love, the way they may be disconnected from love, or the way they express love. Where does love lie in all these relationships? In what way do you love? What if it is not about how much love you get, but how much you give? Look deep into yourself, your fears, hopes, and desires you hold for love in other people, and when you see you are not that different, then love can blossom like a flower. You will feel connected, loved, and satisfied, even in the face of misfortune. Now tune in to yourself. Reach that place of *I want to be loved, and I fear I will not be.* This is a dark place. It probably has been there a very long time. Conceivably a parent, family member, lover, or someone else heightened it. However, it is a scar you bear. No one inflicted it. It is yours, and if it is yours, then you can heal it. As you are the one holding on to it, you are the one that can let it go.

We hold on to sufferings, feeling fragile about them, as they shape our identities and mold who we are. As we grow older, we must be able to let go and move beyond these hostile identities so we may rise into wholeness. This will only occur when we understand the pains we carry, how they are produced from ignorance, just like when others hurt us, their behavior is derived from ignorance. When we learn to be compassionate with our ignorance, we will be more sympathetic of the ignorance in others.

There's a deep place within us where we fear that we will never be loved. Sometimes, around that childlike and brittle feeling is abandoned hopelessness. Trust that this will not last. Beyond all these wounded, dry, and empty deserts is a well of everlasting love. The decency of life is unearthed within the most forsaken pits if you allow yourself to open up, patiently, to the cherry blossom. The force of life will always surface and without compromise.

If we could look into each other's hearts and
understand the unique challenges each of us faces, I
think we would treat each other much more gently,
with more love, patience, tolerance, and care.

— Marvin J. Ashton

Behind your fear of not being loved is love. This embodiment of fear itself is love, as it bestows your humanity to you, your potential for openness, your willingness to accept new ideas or suggestions, that I can only call harmony—the force that is ahead of our ego's grip and judgment. When you are ready to be patient, to rest in stillness, silently, without a struggle over this fear of not being loved, you will discover enormous creativity. In a way, it is the key to the psyche that drives you from the grasp of your ego into God's kingdom, heaven. Rest there, and you will find love, and it will conquer all.

For anything worth having one must pay the price; and the price is always work, patience, love, self-sacrifice—no paper currency, no promises to pay, but the gold of real service. John Burroughs

At the bottom of patience, one finds heaven. Kanuri

So, endure patiently, with beautiful patience. Quran, CH70: V5.

✳ ✳ ✳

BONUS CHAPTER:
THE MESSENGER'S PROPHECY

*The lies (Western slander) which well-meaning
zeal has heaped round this man (Muhammad)
are disgraceful to ourselves only.*

—Thomas Carlyle

Multiple reasons inspired me to write about Prophet Muhammad. The main one is the global misconception of his message that not only slandered his real character but alienated a dominant religion that was ultimately grounded in peace and love. If you study this noble man's nature and intentions, you'll realize that some of his followers abused his message. It's one thing to judge a religion based on the messenger and another to judge it based on led-astray and misguided believers. Imagine engaging in the game 'broken telephone'; this is precisely what happened when he attempted to deliver his revelations and pass them on to generations. *Islam* means surrender, to God. That statement alone is self-explanatory; it requires a complete disconnection from the materialistic world. The very same person that was (and still is) accused as a warlord, only went to battles to defend his faith. He vehemently went to war to defend his immense belief in leading people to a world free of materialism. He was the only person in history that fought, not for the sake of money, rewards, spoils, land, legacy, or materialistic possessions. He went to war to defend humankind from their egoistic selves with a motive to consider their unity with the divine creator.

Now, Muslims believe in all the prophets that preceded him; needless to say, all God's messengers held the same messages whether they were Jesus, Moses, Buddha, and so on. They all inspired people in different regions and cultures in various ways to address the truth of the divine oneness of God and us. To Muslims, Prophet Muhammad is the final prophet to conclude the spiritual revelation and mark the beginning of an awakening. As we learn about more scientific discoveries, we somehow manage to find similar explanations for it in the Quran. I began to realize why the whole concept of embracing faith is so important. To have faith in the unknown is no different from believing in science. They are both undiscovered and entangled. We will never reach a stage where we know it all; however, there is no reason for us not to question existence, life, and everything around us and be open to any possibility.

The first revelation on Prophet Muhammad was the word *Read*. The Prophet was illiterate, yet he passed on miraculous prophecies, doctrines, and inspirations to humanity. Science and religion do not clash, not one bit. For instance, nothing in the Quran refutes the big bang theory. It's very much supported, and I have no idea how this theory was separated from religion. And who decided that? Many of the definitions that people derive from religion are misinterpreted, and this is quite obvious as many terms, expressions, and declarations can be transmuted into numerous meanings, leaving everything open-ended and subject to discovery. Otherwise, what are we here for?

Prophet Muhammad used to regularly hike Mount Al-Nur (Mountain of the Light) and meditate alone in the dark. When he turned forty, he began having visions and hearing voices during his sleep. Searching for certainty, he would meditate at Mount Hira, near Mecca. During these times, the Archangel Gabriel appeared to him in his sleep and instructed him to recite *In the name of the Lord*. This was the first of numerous revelations that became the foundation of the Quran. These initial messages denoted the existence of one creator, contradicting the polytheistic beliefs of the pre-Islamic Arabian Peninsula. Records of the Prophet's ascension (mi'raj) have overwhelmed the imaginations of writers and artists for centuries. One night, during the Prophet's sleep, the Archangel Gabriel came to him and instructed him, "Read" then led him on a journey of knowledge about the creation of the universe. Mounted on the blissful horse Buraq, Prophet Muhammad migrated from the Ka'ba in Mecca to the Farthest Mosque, which Muslims consider to be Al-Aqsa Mosque in Jerusalem. When he arrived there, he prayed with other prophets such as Abraham, Moses, and Jesus, and then ascended to the skies, where Gabriel accompanied him through heaven and hell, then finally came face-to-face with God. After that, he returned to earth to recapitulate and spread the message of God.

Studies nowadays reveal that meditation in a quiet and dark place can stimulate the production of DMT (Di-methyltryptamine) in the pineal gland. That is the very substance responsible for dream states, NDE, and psychedelic trips that connect us to the spirit realm. It's plausible that stillness and meditation inhibit the function of MAOIs, thus transporting you to an unusual dimensional state, just like yogis report in kundalini yoga. It is possible that Prophet Muhammad, along with so many other spiritual messengers, was able to reach this state where he did communicate with spiritual beings that provided him with messages—messages that we can't fully decode because we have not reached that degree of spirituality yet. In this Aquarian age, we have reached a stage where people report their DMT experiences and encounters with beings in different dimensions that help enlighten them and send back messages to ameliorate themselves and the rest of humanity. How is this different than what we once considered a parable? Dr. William Draper wrote, "Four years after the death of Justinian, AD 569, was born in Mecca, in Arabia, the man who, of all men, has exercised the greatest influence upon the human race... To be the religious head of many empires, to guide the daily life of one-third of the human race, may perhaps justify the title of a Messenger of God."

The purpose of Islam is to surrender to God; it's not to punish the infidels, preach aggressively, or kill the nonbelievers. Life is a journey, and it's our responsibility only to search for the truth. Islam is part of a journey. A quest to surrender to the divine entirely doesn't happen overnight. We were given a masterpiece of a brain to be able to read, educate ourselves, and search for the truth, not blindly follow. It's our choice to do whatever we want to do, and it's our choice to become who we wish to become, but at the end of the day we have been shown what's right from what's wrong, and we'll intuitively know it deep within our hearts and souls after grasping the whole truth. The concept of heaven and hell are imbued concepts we do not understand but have to be pierced to chastise the ego-self; otherwise, we'll be living in a chaotic world. Who knows if heaven or hell are final destinations? For all we know, we could be

living it, and the afterlife is something utterly foreign to our imagination. Try asking a volunteer who has had a DMT-induced experience, Ayahuasca, or a near-death experience to describe what they
saw, felt, and experienced, and they will never be able to describe
it accurately. So how are we supposed to describe heaven when we
can't even describe love?

The reason Islam is regarded as the irrevocable religion is that
it's indeed considered a journey, a mission of purification. Mind
that many people assume that quite a few contradictions subsist in
the Holy Book when in fact it's based on a time line, an expedition
recounted over twenty-three years. To believe in other religions
makes you a believer as well, not an outcast. However, the whole
point of Islam being the definitive destination is that it guides the
human soul to achieve full submission to God's will and to put
his health, wealth, and trust in the oneness of this universe. Now,
whether to follow it or not and to connect with God and the self
is entirely your decision to make. No one is in a position to judge
another because religion is a personal spiritual guide, and it's most
certainly a journey of knowledge and understanding. The Prophet
himself was on a spiritual journey his entire life and only was introduced to the Quranic verses and revelations when he reached the age
of forty. Pure enlightenment is knowing the truth at any stage of *your*
time line, as long as it leads you to the inevitable spiritual surrender.

I leave you with some thoughts from several historical figures,
including some Easterners and Westerners, who wrote what they
truly believed about Prophet Muhammad.

I wanted to know the best of the life of one who holds
today an undisputed sway over the hearts of millions of
mankind... I became more than ever convinced that it

was not the sword that won a place for Islam in those days in the scheme of life. It was the rigid simplicity, the utter self-effacement of the Prophet, the scrupulous regard for pledges, his intense devotion to his friends and followers, his intrepidity, his fearlessness, his absolute trust in God and in his own mission. These and not the sword carried everything before them and surmounted every obstacle. When I closed the second volume (of the Prophet's biography) I was sorry there was not more for me to read of that great life.

— Mahatma Gandhi

I have always held the religion of Muhammad in high estimation because of its wonderful vitality. It is the only religion which appears to me to possess that assimilating capacity to the changing phase of existence which can make itself appeal to every age. I have studied him—the wonderful man and in my opinion, far from being an anti-Christ, he must be called the Savior of Humanity.

— George Bernard Shaw

His readiness to undergo persecution for his beliefs, the high moral character of the men who believed in him and looked up to him as a leader, and the greatness of his ultimate achievement—all argue his fundamental integrity. To suppose Muhammad an impostor raises more problems than it solves. Moreover, none of the great figures of history is so poorly appreciated in the West as Muhammad. Thus, not merely must we credit Muhammad with essential honesty

and integrity of purpose, if we are to understand him at
all; if we are to correct the errors we have inherited from
the past, we must not forget the conclusive proof is a much
stricter requirement than a show of plausibility, and in a
matter, such as this only to be attained with difficulty.

— W. Montgomery Watt

If greatness of purpose, smallness of means, and astonishing
results are the three criteria of a human genius, who could
dare compare any great man in history with Muhammad?
The most famous men created arms, laws, and empires only.
They founded, if anything at all, no more than material
powers which often crumbled away before their eyes.
This man moved not only armies, legislations, empires,
peoples, dynasties, but millions of men in one-third of
the then inhabited world; and more than that, he moved
the altars, the gods, the religions, the ideas, the beliefs,
and the souls. He founded upon a book of which each
letter has become a law, a spiritual nationality embracing
people of all languages and races; and made an indelible
imprint upon this Muslim nation, for the hatred of false
gods and the passion for the God, One and Immaterial.

— Alphonse de LaMartine

The personality of Muhammad, it is most difficult to get
into the whole truth of it. Only a glimpse of it I can catch.
What a dramatic succession of picturesque scenes! There is
Muhammad, the Prophet; there is Muhammad, the Warrior;

Muhammad, the Businessman; Muhammad, the Statesman; Muhammad, the Orator; Muhammad, the Reformer; Muhammad, the Refuge of Orphans; Muhammad, the Protector of Slaves; Muhammad, the Emancipator of Women; Muhammad, the Judge; Muhammad, the Saint. All in all these magnificent roles, in all these departments of human activities, he is like a hero.

—K. S. Ramakrishna Rao

It is impossible for anyone who studies the life and character of the great Prophet of Arabia, who knew how he taught and how he lived, to feel anything but reverence for that mighty Prophet, one of the great messengers of the Supreme. And although in what I put to you I shall say many things which may be familiar to many, yet I myself feel, whenever I reread them, a new way of admiration, a new sense of reverence for that mighty Arabian teacher.

— Annie Besant

It was the first religion that preached and practiced democracy; for in the mosque, when the call for prayer is sounded, and worshippers are gathered together, the democracy of Islam is embedded five times a day when the peasant and king kneel side by side and proclaim: "God alone is great"… I have been struck over and over again by this indivisible unity of Islam that makes man instinctively and equally a brother.

— Sarojini Naidu

Serious or trivial, his daily behavior instituted a canon which millions observe this day with conscious memory. No one regarded by any section of the human race as Perfect Man has ever been imitated minutely. The conduct of the founder of Christianity has not governed the ordinary life of his followers. Forever, no founder of a religion has left on so solitary an eminence as the Muslim apostle.

— D. G. Hogarth

Muhammad does not consider God as a human being and never makes himself equal to God. Muslims worship nothing except God and Muhammad is his Messenger. There is not any mystery and secret in it.

— Leo Tolstoy

The End

WORK CITATIONS

Al-Sulaiti, G. (2019, February 26). Personal communication.

Albert Einstein Quotes. (n.d.). BrainyQuote.com. Retrieved March 29, 2019, from BrainyQuote.com Web site: https://www.brainyquote.com/ quotes/albert_einstein_161289.

Albert Schweitzer Quotes. (n.d.). QuoteFancy.com. Retrieved March 29, 2019, from QuoteFancy.com Web site: https://quotefancy.com/ quote/764576/Albert-Schweitzer-Happiness-is-the-only-thing-that-multiplies-when-you-share-it.

Aleister Crowley Quotes. (n.d.). BrainyQuote.com. Retrieved March 30, 2019, from BrainyQuote.com Web site: https://www.brainyquote.com/ quotes/aleister_crowley_156787.

Alexander, E. (2012). *"Proof of Heaven: A Neurosurgeon's Journey into the Afterlife"*. New York: Simon & Schuster.

ALICE. (n.d.). AliceInfo.com. Retrieved March 29, 2019, from www. AliceInfo.com Web site: http://aliceinfo.cern.ch/public/welcome.html.

Ashton, M. (n.d.). GoodReads.com. Retrieved March 29, 2019, from GoodReads.com Web site: https://www.goodreads.com/ quotes/51853-if-we-could-look-into-each-other-s-hearts-and-understand.

Atlas Experiment. (n.d.). AtlasExperiment.com. Retrieved March 29, 2019, from www.AtlasExperiment.com Web site: http://atlasexperiment. org.

Bachhuber, D.R., Love, G.D., Ryff, **C.D.**, Davidson, R.J. (2012). Conscientiousness predicts greater recovery from negative emotion. *Emotion*. Retrieved March 29, 2019, from psycnet.apa.org.

Bale, C. (2019, January 6). Christian Bale Thanks SATAN in Acceptance Speech at Golden Globe 2019 Award [video file]. Posted to https://www. youtube.com/watch?v=pJxFi0sbLww.

Behary, W. (2008). *"Disarming the Narcissist"*. California: New Harbinger Publications.

Benjamin Franklin Quotes. (n.d.). BrainyQuote.com. Retrieved March 30, 2019, from BrainyQuote.com Web site: https://www.brainyquote.com/ quotes/benjamin_franklin_151645.

Besant, A. (n.d.). IslamForChristians.com. Retrieved March 29, 2019, from IslamForChristians.com Web site: http://www.islamforchristians. com/say-prophet-muhammad/.

Billy Graham Quotes. (n.d.). BrainyQuote.com. Retrieved March 30, 2019, from BrainyQuote.com Web site: https://www.brainyquote.com/quotes/ billy_graham_626358.

Bhat, R.A., Murtaza, S.T., Sharique, M., Jabin, F. (2014). Unity of Health Through Yoga And Islamic Prayer 'Salah'. Academic Sports Scholar. Volume 3, Issue 10, Pages 2-6.

Blanco, O. (1996). *"Preparation for the Personal Ayahuasca Experience"*

Retrieved March 29, 2019 from http://biopark.org/prepara-tion-and-cleansing.html.

Campbell, K. (2005). *"When You Love a Man Who Loves Himself"*. Illinois: Sourcebooks, Inc.

Campbell, K. (2009). *"The Narcissism Epidemic"*. New York: Free Press.

Carlyle T. (1841). "On Heroes, Hero Worship and the Heroic in History". Scotland: James Fraser.

Catherine Pulsifer Quotes. (n.d.). Wow4u.com. Retrieved March 30, 2019, from Wow4u.com Web site: https://www.wow4u.com/patience/.

Chainey, G. (1995). *"A Literary History of Cambridge"*. United Kingdom: Cambridge University Press Bartleby.com. Retrieved March 30, 2019, from

https://books.google.com.qa/books?isbn=052147681X.

Chalmers, I., Altman, D.G. (1999). The Lancet. Retrieved March 29, 2019, from https://www.thelancet.com.

Corbin, H. (n.d.). Displate.com. Retrieved March 29, 2019, from Displate.com Web site: https://displate.com/displate/259922.

Corsten, F. (2016, June 14). Ferry Corsten presents Gouryella - Neba [Official Music Video]

[video file]. Posted to https://www.youtube.com/watch?v=y8qHw2ohPxQ.

Corsten, F. (2015, June 18). Ferry Corsten presents Gouryella – Anahera [Official Music Video]

[video file]. Posted to https://www.youtube.com/watch?v=7ZMZHbAKvGA.

Crandell, J. (n.d.). Medium.com. Retrieved March 29, 2019, from Medium.com Web site: https://medium.com/@wadesmith848/the-nature-of-yoga-is-to-shine-the-light-of-awareness-into-the-darkest-corners-of-the-body-701d5adb726.

Crowley, A. (1912). *"The Book of Lies"*. United Kingdom: Babes of the Abyss.

Crowley, A. (1913). "Magick, Liber ABA, Book 4". Newburyport, Massachusetts: Red Wheel Weiser Conari.

Crowley, A. (1922). "Diary of a Drug Fiend". United Kingdom: Sirius.

Crowley, A. (1944). "The Book of Thoth". Newburyport, Massachusetts: Weiser Books.

Davis, A.K., Barsulglia, J.P., Lancelotta, R., Grant, R.M., & Renn, E. (2018). The epidemiology of 5-methyoxy-N, N-dimethyltryptamine (5-MeO-DMT) use: Benefits, consequences, patterns of use, subjective uses, and reasons for consumption. Journal of Psychopharmacology, Volume 32(7), Pages 779-792.

Darwin, C. (1859). "The Origin of Species". London, United Kingdom: John Murray.

Dickerson, K. (2014, September 8). "Stephen Hawking Says 'God Particle' Could Wipe Out the Universe". *Live Science*. Retrieved from https://www.livescience.com/47737-stephen-hawking-higgs-boson-universe-doomsday.html.

Draper W. (1863). "History of Intellectual Development of Europe". New York: Harper Brothers Publishers.

Eckhart Tolle Quotes. (n.d.). BrainyQuote.com. Retrieved March 29, 2019, from BrainyQuote.com Web site: https://www.brainyquote.com/quotes/eckhart_tolle_571602.

Einstein, A. (n.d.). GoodReads.com. Retrieved March 29, 2019, from GoodReads.com Web site: https://www.goodreads.com/quotes/282814-the-most-beautiful-thing-we-can-experience-is-the-mysterious.

Elleithy, H. (2019). PicDeer.com. Retrieved March 29, 2019, from PicDeer. com Web site: http://picdeer.com/hana_leithyy.

Elshazly, M. (2019, March 3). Personal interview.

Erwin Schrodinger Quotes. (n.d.). BrainyQuote.com. Retrieved March 29, 2019, from BrainyQuote.com Web site: https://www.brainyquote.com/ quotes/erwin_schrodinger_304795.

Etnikas Editors. (n.d.). *"Inca Religion and Ayahuasca"*. Retrieved March 29, 2019 from https://www.etnikas.com/inca-religion.

Fortlage, L., Puleo, E., Benson, H. (1995). The relaxation Response. *Medicine & Science*. Retrieved March 29, 2019, from psycnet.apa.org.

Frederic N., Gerald, J. M., Dun-Xian, T. (2018). Melatonin in Heart Failure: A Promising Therapeutic Strategy? *Molecules*. Volume 23(7): 1819.

Friesen, Rozenek, R., Clippinger, K. (2011). Bone mineral density and body composition of collegiate modern dancers. *Journal of Dance Medicine & Science*, Volume 15, Number 1, Pages 31-36(6).

Gandi, M. (n.d.). FlipForInspiration.com. Retrieved March 29, 2019, from FlipForInspiration.com Web site: https://flipforinspiration.wordpress. com/2013/12/20/earth-provides-enough-to-satisfy-every-mans-need-but-not-every-mans-greed-gandhi/.

Gandhi, M. (n.d.). Goodreads.com. Retrieved March 29, 2019, from GoodReads.com Web site:

https://www.goodreads.com/ quotes/936395-i-wanted-to-know-the-best-of-the-life-of.

Gates, R. (n.d.). Medium.com. Retrieved March 29, 2019, from Medium.com Web site: https://medium.com/@VernonFoster/ yoga-its-not-a-work-out-it-s-a-work-in-5b53b7841faa.

Grayling A. (n.d.). "A quasi-political Explanation of the Higgs Boson; for Mr Waldegrave, UK Science Minister 1993.". *Course Hero* on BBC.doc. Retrieved from https://www.coursehero.com/file/p22nh4r/The-knock-on-benefits-to-the-whole-of-science-and-medicine-to-society-at-large/.

Grey, A. (n.d.). The Emotion Machine. Retrieved March 29, 2019 from https://www.theemotionmachine.com/best-self-improvement-articles/.

Harriet Tubman Quotes. (n.d.). BrainyQuote.com. Retrieved March 30, 2019, from BrainyQuote.com Web site: https://www.brainyquote.com/quotes/harriet_tubman_310306.

Harris, S. (n.d.). *"In his blog"*. Retrieved March 29, 2019 from https://en.wikipedia.org/wiki/Eben_Alexander_(author).

Helen Rowland Quotes. (n.d.). BrainyQuote.com. Retrieved March 30, 2019, from BrainyQuote.com Web site: https://www.brainyquote.com/quotes/helen_rowland_379364.

Henry Wadsworth Longfellow Quotes. (n.d.). BrainyQuote.com. Retrieved March 30, 2019, from BrainyQuote.com Web site: https://www.brainy-quote.com/quotes/henry_wadsworth_longfello_118043.

History.com Editors. (2017, September 13). The Devil. *History*. Retrieved from https://www.history.com/topics/folklore/history-of-the-devil.

Hogarth, D.G. (n.d.). CyberIstan.com. Retrieved March 29, 2019, from CyberIstan.com Web site: http://www.cyberistan.org/islamic/quote1.html.

Home.Cern Editors. (n.d.). "Pulling together: Superconducting electromagnets". Home.Cern. Retrieved from https://home.cern/science/engineering/pulling-together-superconducting-electromagnets.

Howell, J. (n.d.). Forbes.com. Retrieved March 29, 2019, from Forbes.com Web site https://www.forbes.com/global/2005/0725/064.html* * *2e705dbf7ce0.

Institute of Medical Psychology, Centre for Psychosocial Medicine, Heidelberg University, Bergheimer Strasse 20, 69115 Heidelberg, Germany. (2012, March 23) *Ayahuasca and the process of regulation in Brazil and internationally: implications and challenges.* Int J Drug Policy. Volume (2), Pages154-161.

Iyengar, B. K. S. (n.d.). GoodReads.com. Retrieved March 29, 2019, from GoodReads.com Web site: https://www.goodreads.com/author/quotes/78286.B_K_S_Iyengar.

Iyengar, B. K. S. (n.d.). GoodReads.com. Retrieved March 29, 2019, from Light on Life. Web site: https://www.goodreads.com/quotes/800463-you-must-purge-yourself-before-finding-faults-in-others-when.

Iyengar, B. K. S. (n.d.). Medium.com. Retrieved March 29, 2019, from Medium.com Web site:

https://medium.com/@arthiramesh/seven-life-lessons-from-an-iyengar-yoga-retreat-f8877f0a3db6.

John Burroughs Quotes. (n.d.). BrainyQuote.com. Retrieved March 30, 2019, from BrainyQuote.com Web site: https://www.brainyquote.com/quotes/john_burroughs_150290.

John Quincy Adams Quotes. (n.d.). BrainyQuote.com. Retrieved March 30, 2019, from BrainyQuote.com Web site: https://www.brainyquote.com/quotes/john_quincy_adams_387094.

John Wooden Quotes. (n.d.). BrainyQuote.com. Retrieved March 29, 2019, from BrainyQuote.com Web site: https://www.brainyquote.com/quotes/john_wooden_120997.

Johns Hopkins Institute. (1996). Psychedelic Research Unit. Retrieved March 29, 2019 from https://hopkinspsychedelic.org.

Johnson, M.W., Richards, W.A., & Griffiths, R.R. (2008). Human hallu-
cinogen research: guidelines for safety. Journal of Psychopharmacology,
Volume 22(6), Pages 603-620.

Joyce Meyer Quotes. (n.d.). BrainyQuote.com. Retrieved March 30, 2019,
from BrainyQuote.com Web site: https://www.brainyquote.com/quotes/
joyce_meyer_567645.

Julie Weiland Quotes. (n.d.). AhimsaYogaStudios.com. Retrieved March
29, 2019, from AhimsaYogaStudios.com Website: https://www.ahimsayo-
gastudios.com/blog/motivational-yoga-quotes.

Julius Caesar Quotes. (n.d.). BrainyQuote.com. Retrieved March 30, 2019,
from BrainyQuote.com Web site: https://www.brainyquote.com/quotes/
julius_caesar_135052.

Jung, C.G., Read, H.E., Fordham, H., Adler, G. (1953). Routledge and K.
Paul The Collected Works: General index to The collected works of CG
Jung/compiled by Barbara Forryan and Janet M. Glover.

Kahlil Gibran Quotes. (n.d.). BrainyQuote.com. Retrieved March 29, 2019,
from BrainyQuote.com Web site: https://www.brainyquote.com/quotes/
khalil_gibran_136982.

Kanuri Quotes. (n.d.). WisdomQuotes.com. Retrieved March 30,
2019, from WisdomQuotes.com Web site http://wisdomquotes.com/
patience-quotes/.

Kempton, S. (2017). YogaSpot.nl. Retrieved March 29, 2019, from
YogaSpot.nl Web site: https://yogaspot.nl/kwetsbaarheid-in-yoga/.

King Jr., M. L. (n.d.). Leighb.com. Retrieved March 29, 2019, from www.
leighb.com Web site: http://www.leighb.com/MLK_Interrelated.htm.

Knapton, S. (2015, March 23). "Big Bang theory could be debunked by
Large Hadron Collider". The Telegraph. Retrieved from https://www.

telegraph.co.uk/news/science/large-hadron-collider/11489442/Big-Bang-theory-could-be-debunked-by-Large-Hadron-Collider.html.

Krauss, L. (2012, January 10). *"A Universe from Nothing: Why There Is Something Rather than Nothing"*. New York: Free Press.

Lamartine, A. (n.d.). WikiQuote.com. Retrieved March 29, 2019, from WikiQuote.com Web site: https://en.wikiquote.org/wiki/Alphonse_de_Lamartine.

Lipton, B. (2013). *"The Honeymoon Effect: The Science of Creating Heaven on Earth"*. California: Hay House Inc.

Lucius Annaeus Seneca Quotes. (n.d.). BrainyQuote.com. Retrieved March 29, 2019, from BrainyQuote.com Web site: https://www.brainyquote.com/quotes/lucius_annaeus_seneca_155016.

Marquez, G. G. (n.d.). Goodreads.com. Retrieved March 29, 2019, from GoodReads.com Web site: https://www.goodreads.com/quotes/51938-sex-is-the-consolation-you-have-when-you-can-t-have.

Max Planck Quotes. (n.d.). BrainyQuote.com. Retrieved March 29, 2019, from BrainyQuote.com Web site: https://www.brainyquote.com/quotes/max_planck_211839.

McBride, K. (2015). *"Will I Ever Be Free of You"*. New York: Atria Books.

McManus, E. (2006). "Soul Cravings: An Exploration of the Human Spirit". Nashville, Tennessee: Thomas Nelson.

Melody Beattie Quotes. (n.d.). BrainyQuote.com. Retrieved March 29, 2019, from BrainyQuote.com Web site: https://www.brainyquote.com/quotes/melody_beattie_177949.

Miller, J., O'Donnell J. (2016). Executive suicides scratch Switzerland's picture perfect veneer. *Reuters*.

Milne, A. (n.d.). GoodReads.com. Retrieved March 29, 2019, from GoodReads.com Web site: https://www.goodreads.com/quotes/210608-rivers-know-this-there-is-no-hurry-we-shall-get.

Mipham, S. (2012). "Running with the Mind of Meditation: Lessons for Training Body and Mind". New York: Harmony.

Moliere Quotes. (n.d.). BrainyQuote.com. Retrieved March 30, 2019, from BrainyQuote.com Web site: https://www.brainyquote.com/quotes/moliere_378425.

Naidu, S. (n.d.). IslamCity.com. Retrieved March 29, 2019, from IslamCity.com Web site: https://www.islamicity.org/5650/muhammad-the-prophet/.

NASAexplores. (2004, May 20). "Astronauts take a Dive." Retrieved March 29, 2019 from https://www.nasa.gov/audience/foreducators/9-12/features/F_Astronauts_Take_Dive.html.

Page, L. (2009, November 6). 'Something may come through' dimensional 'doors' at LHC. The Register. Retrieved from https://www.theregister.co.uk/2009/11/06/lhc_dimensional_portals/.

Papp, M.E., Wändell, P.E., Lindfors, P., Nygren-Bonnier, M., Eur, J. (2017). Effects of yogic exercises on functional capacity, lung function and quality of life in participants with obstructive pulmonary. Phys Rehabil Med. Volume 53(3), Pages 447-461.

Papp, M.E., Henriques, M., Biguet, G., Wändell, P.E., Nygren-Bonnier, M. J., Bodyw, M. T. (2018). Experiences of hatha yogic exercises among patients with obstructive pulmonary diseases: A qualitative study. Volume 22(4), Pages 896-903.

Papp, M.E., Lindfors, P., Nygren-Bonnier, M., Gullstrand, L., Wändell, P.E. (2016). Effects of High-Intensity Hatha Yoga on Cardiovascular Fitness, Adipocytokines, and Apolipoproteins in Healthy Students: A Randomized Controlled Study. Complement Med. Volume 22(1), Pages 81-87.

Papp, M.E., Lindfors, P., Storck, N., Wändell, P.E. (2013). Increased heart rate variability but no effect on blood pressure from 8 weeks of hatha yoga - a pilot study. *BMC Res Notes*. Volume 11. Pages 6-59.

Peterson, J. (2017, May 17). Jordan Peterson – The Mystery of DMT and Psilocybin [video file]. Posted to https://www.youtube.com/watch?v=Gol5sPM073k&t=197s.

Piper, M. (n.d.). *"Daughters of Narcissistic Mothers"*. Retrieved March 29, 2019 from *The 7 Steps to Recovering from a Narcissistic Mother*. Website: https://space.mit.edu/LIGO/more.html.

Prasetyo, D.F. (2015). Journal Riset Mahasiswa Bimbingan Dan, Retrieved March 29, 2019 from journal.student.uny.ac.id.

Ralph Waldo Emerson Quotes. (n.d.). BrainyQuote.com. Retrieved March 30, 2019, from BrainyQuote.com Web site: https://www.brainyquote.com/quotes/ralph_waldo_emerson_106883.

Rao, K.S. (n.d.). GoodReads.com. Retrieved March 29, 2019, from GoodReads.com Web site:

https://www.goodreads.com/quotes/802710-the-personality-of-muhammad-it-is-most-difficult-to-get.

Richard Bach Quotes. (n.d.). BrainyQuote.com. Retrieved March 29, 2019, from BrainyQuote.com Web site: https://www.brainyquote.com/quotes/richard_bach_132675.

Robbins, T. (n.d.). GoodReads.com. Retrieved March 29, 2019, from GoodReads.com Web site: https://www.goodreads.com/quotes/877199-the-only-impossible-journey-is-the-one-you-never-begin.

Robert, W. M., Christopher, M. S. (2008), Scholarpedia, 3(4):3313

Ruiz, D. M. (1999). *The Mastery of Love: A Practical Guide to the Art of Relationship --Toltec Wisdom Book"*. San Rafael, California: Amber-Allen Publishing.

Rumi. (n.d.). GoodReads.com. Retrieved March 29, 2019, from GoodReads.com Web site: https://www.goodreads.com/quotes/723832-you-have-to-keep-breaking-your-heart-until-it-opens.

Rumi. (n.d.). GoodReads.com. Retrieved March 29, 2019, from GoodReads.com Web site: https://www.goodreads.com/quotes/7440878-there-is-a-voice-that-doesn-t-use-words-listen.

Rumi. (n.d.). GoodReads.com. Retrieved March 29, 2019, from GoodReads.com Web site: https://www.goodreads.com/quotes/968628-patience-is-not-sitting-and-waiting-it-is-foreseeing-it.

Rumi Quotes. (n.d.). BrainyQuote.com. Retrieved March 29, 2019, from BrainyQuote.com Web site: https://www.brainyquote.com/quotes/rumi_597889.

Sadghuru Tweets. (2017). Twitter.com. Retrieved March 29, 2019, from Twitter.com Web site: https://twitter.com/sadhgurujv/status/901636660403765248?lang=en.

Saeed, S.A., Antonacci, D.J. (2010). Exercise, yoga, and meditation for depressive and anxiety disorders. *American family*. Retrieved March 29, 2019, from search.ebscohost.com.

Sahih Al-Bukhari Book 01. Revelation. (n.d.). HadithCollection.com. Retrieved March 29, 2019, from www.HadithCollection.com Web site: http://hadithcollection.com/sahihbukhari/sahih-bukhari-book-01-revelation.html.

Saint Augustine Quotes. (n.d.). BrainyQuote.com. Retrieved March 30, 2019, from BrainyQuote.com Web site: https://www.brainyquote.com/quotes/saint_augustine_108487.

Saint Augustine Quotes. (n.d.). BrainyQuote.com. Retrieved March 29, 2019, from BrainyQuote.com Web site: https://www.brainyquote.com/ quotes/saint_augustine_148546.

Sassoli de Bianchi, M. (2013). Quantum Dice. *Annals of Physics*, Volume 336, Pages 56-75.

Saswato R. (2013, March 26). "How the Higgs Boson Might Spell Doom for the Universe". *Scientific American*. Retrieved from https://www.scientificamerican.com/article/ how-the-higgs-boson-might-spell-doom-for-the-universe/.

Schiffmann, E. (n.d.). QuoteFancy.com. Retrieved March 29, 2019, from QuoteFancy.com Web site: https://quotefancy.com/quote/1711563/ Erich-Schiffmann-Yoga-ia-a-way-of-moving-into-stillness-in-order-to-experience-the-truth.

Schrodinger, E. (n.d.). AzQuotes.com. Retrieved March 29, 2019, from AzQuotes.com Web site: https://www.azquotes.com/quote/851832.

Shaw, B. (n.d.). Goodreads.com. Retrieved March 29, 2019, from GoodReads.com Web site:

https://www.goodreads.com/ quotes/3227488-i-have-always-held-the-religion-of-muhammad-in-high.

Solomon Ibn Gabirol Quotes. (n.d.). BrainyQuote.com. Retrieved March 30, 2019, from BrainyQuote.com Web site: https://www.brainyquote.com/ quotes/solomon_ibn_gabirol_164759.

Space.Mit Editors. (n.d.). "*Laser Interferometer Gravitational Wave Observatory*". Compiled by MIT LIGO. Retrieved March 29, 2019 from https://space.mit.edu/LIGO/more.html.

Spitzer, R.L., Williams, J.B.W. (1980). *Diagnostic and statistical manual of mental disorders*. American psychiatric association- Citeseer.

Stovall, J. (2014). "Wisdom for Winners, A Millionaire Mindset". New York: Sound Wisdom.

Strassman, R. (2000). *"DMT: The Spirit Molecule: A Doctor's Revolutionary Research Into the Biology of Near-Death and Mystical Experiences"*. Rochester, Vermont: Inner Traditions/Bear & Company.

Tabrezi. S. (n.d.). GoodReads.com. Retrieved March 29, 2019, from GoodReads.com Web site: https://www.goodreads.com/quotes/6751415-don-t-search-for-heaven-and-hell-in-the-future-both.

Taub, B. (n.d.). Do Our Brains Produce DMT, And If So, Why? *Beckley Foundation*.

Tecumseh Quotes. (n.d.). BrainyQuote.com. Retrieved March 29, 2019, from BrainyQuote.com Web site: https://www.brainyquote.com/quotes/tecumseh_190018.

Thoene. B. (n.d.). GoodReads.com. Retrieved March 29, 2019, from GoodReads.com Web site: https://www.goodreads.com/quotes/364077-what-is-right-is-often-forgotten-by-what-is-convenient.

Tolstoy, L. (n.d.). GoodReads.com. Retrieved March 29, 2019, from GoodReads.com Web site: https://www.goodreads.com/quotes/688860-patience-is-waiting-not-passively-waiting-that-is-laziness-but.

Tolstoy, L. (n.d.). GoodReads.com. Retrieved March 29, 2019, from GoodReads.com Web site: https://www.goodreads.com/quotes/tag/muhammad.

Tyson, N. D. (n.d.). GoodReads.com. Retrieved March 29, 2019 from https://www.goodreads.com/quotes/484586-the-atoms-of-our-bodies-are-traceable-to-stars-that.

Tzu, L. (n.d.). GoodReads.com. Retrieved March 29, 2019,
from GoodReads.com Web site: https://www.goodreads.com/
quotes/2926-be-content-with-what-you-have-rejoice-in-the-way.

Vaden, T. (2018, April 5). Heraldsun.com. Retrieved March 29, 2019, from
www.HearldSun.com Web site: https://www.heraldsun.com/opinion/arti-
cle207973044.html.

Vaknin, S. (2001). *"Malignant Self-Love: Narcissism Revisited"*. United
Kingdom: Narcissus Publishing.

Verjee, M. (2019, March 11). Personal communication.

Walsch, N. D. (n.d.). GoodReads.com. Retrieved March 29, 2019 from
https://www.goodreads.com/quotes/1011513-quantum-physics-tells-us-
that-nothing-that-is-observed-is.

Waheed, N. (n.d.). GoodReads.com. Retrieved March 29, 2019,
from GoodReads.com Web site: https://www.goodreads.com/
quotes/887726-if-the-ocean-can-calm-itself-so-can-you-we.

Watt, W. (n.d.). GoodReads.com. Retrieved March 29, 2019, from
GoodReads.com Web site:

https://www.goodreads.com/quotes/337640-his-readiness-to-undergo-
persecutions-for-his-beliefs-the-high.

Wayne Dyer Quotes. (n.d.). BrainyQuote.com. Retrieved March 29, 2019,
from BrainyQuote.com Web site: https://www.brainyquote.com/quotes/
wayne_dyer_718093.

WhyIslam Editors. (2014, July 20). WhyIslam.com. *Spiritual Benefits of
Prayers*. Retrieved March 29, 2019, from www.WhyIslam.com Web site:
https://www.whyislam.org/on-faith/spiritual-benefits-of-prayer/.

William Arthur Ward Quotes. (n.d.). QuoteFancy.com. Retrieved March
30, 2019, from QuoteFancy.com Web site: https://quotefancy.com/
quote/933948/William-Arthur-Ward-Today-s-patience-can-transform-
yesterday-s-discouragements-into.

William Penn Quotes. (n.d.). BrainyQuote.com. Retrieved March 30,
2019, from BrainyQuote.com Web site: https://www.brainyquote.com/
quotes/william_penn_121888.

Willigen, M. V. (2000). Differential benefits of volunteering across the life
course. *The Journals of Gerontology Series B*. Retrieved March 29, 2019,
from academic.oup.com.

Yoga International. (n.d.). YogaInternational.com. Retrieved March 29,
2019, from www.Yoga International.com Web site: https://yogainterna-
tional.com/article/view/the-real-meaning-of-meditation.

Zolfagharifard E. (2018, March 14). "Stephen Hawking's final warning to
humanity: Legendary physicist believed we must leave Earth in the next
200 years or face EXTINCTION". *Daily Mail*. Retrieved from https://www.
dailymail.co.uk/sciencetech/article-5498731/Stephen-Hawkings-final-
warning-humanity.html.

Zyga, L. (2015, March 18). "Detection of mini black holes at the LHC
could indicate parallel universes in extra dimensions". Phys.org. Retrieved
from https://phys.org/news/2015-03-mini-black-holes-lhc-parallel.html.